THE SHEPHERD LEADER

Achieving Effective
Shepherding in Your Church

TIMOTHY Z. WITMER

PUBLISHING
P.O. BOX 817 • PHILLIPSBURG • NEW JERSEY 08865-0817

Unless otherwise indicated, Scripture quotations are from the NEW AMERICAN STANDARD BIBLE®. Copyright © 1960, 1962, 1963, 1968, 1971, 1972, 1973, 1975, 1977, 1995 by The Lockman Foundation. Used by permission.

Scripture quotations marked NIV are from the HOLY BIBLE, NEW INTERNATIONAL VERSION®. NIV®. Copyright © 1973, 1978, 1984 by International Bible Society. Used by permission of Zondervan Publishing House. All rights reserved.

Scripture quotations marked ESV are from The Holy Bible, English Standard Version, copyright © 2001 by Crossway Bibles, a division of Good News Publishers. Used by permission. All rights reserved.

Italics within Scripture quotations indicate emphasis added.

Printed in the United States of America

Library of Congress Cataloging-in-Publication Data

Witmer, Timothy Z., 1953-
    The shepherd leader : achieving effective shepherding in your church / Timothy Z. Witmer.
        p. cm.
    Includes bibliographical references and index.
    ISBN 978-1-59638-131-5 (pbk.)
    1. Discipling (Christianity) 2. Elders (Church officers) 3. Christian leadership. I. Title.
BV4520.W538 2010
253--dc22
                                2009047315

To

The officers of Crossroads Community Church (PCA),
who faithfully shepherd the flock of God under their care

and to

Captain Nathan T. Witmer,
who bravely shepherded his troops through the valley of the
shadow of death
Operation Iraqi Freedom

CONTENTS

Part 3: Putting It All Together

FOREWORD

IT IS BOTH an honor and a privilege to be able to write a few words to introduce and commend this very important book.

The Shepherd Leader is just the kind of book that those who know Tim Witmer and his work have been hoping he would write—an intelligent, biblical, balanced, pastoral, sensitive, and realistic exposition of the nature of true leadership in the Christian church. And there is a double bonus: this book is as *readable* as it is *interesting*. Not every study of eldership is as well acquainted with the shepherding practices of the *Nix Besser* sheep farm in rural Pennsylvania as it is with the pastoral care of the human sheep of Kidderminster during the remarkable ministry of Richard Baxter in seventeenth-century England!

This is an intelligent and informative book. Here exegesis and exposition provide a solid biblical foundation. Knowledge of the history of the cure of souls—in Scripture, in the medieval world, the Reformation, right through to the strategies of the great Thomas Chalmers in a deeply deprived urban parish in nineteenth-century Scotland—provides color.

One might expect all this on learning that Dr. Witmer is professor of practical theology at Westminster Seminary in Philadelphia. But what he modestly refrains from underlining in these pages, however, is that he serves simultaneously as the preaching pastor of a vibrant, multicultural Presbyterian church in a highly urbanized community just outside Philadelphia. Under his ministry the hundred-year-old Crossroads Church has been renewed and built up both spiritually and numerically. Indeed, even in its size it equates to what John Owen regarded as ideal for a congregation in which everyone counts, in which gifts abound, but no one is sidelined! Thus long personal experience of pastoral ministry provides relevance and contemporary wisdom. So this is also a wonderfully practical as well as instructive book. It underlines principles that ministers and leaders can employ in the specifics of their own church context, and it provides workable suggestions about how to put them into practice.

These pages have, therefore, been personally test-driven. They do not give us idealistic counsels of perfection that fail to take account of an honest reading of the New Testament and what it teaches us about the condition of Christ's flock. Professor Witmer is too good a theologian to do that. But he is also too caring a pastor not to provide us with approaches to leadership and spiritual care that are practical and workable in all kinds of situations.

To be among the congregation Tim Witmer pastors is—at least in my experience—to sense a little of what it means for sheep to be loved and cared for, well-protected in the flock, and devotedly fed a balanced and healthy diet from God's Word. There is something indefinable, atmospheric about such congregations. It is explicable only in terms of the knowledge of God, faith in and love for Jesus Christ, and a sense of the Spirit's presence. This is what unites the Lord's people together as a family as they worship, pray, and enjoy fellowship together in service and evangelism. Since these things are present in part as a direct fruit of Tim Witmer's ministry and leadership, when he speaks on the subject of pastoral care, we listen. And when he writes about it in this permanent form, we eagerly read. I am personally deeply grateful for our years of friendship, which have given me the opportunity to learn from him, and, in more recent days, for his immediate rapport with and help to the leadership of our congregation.

The reasons *The Shepherd Leader* has these rich and varied qualities—intelligent, biblical, balanced, pastoral, sensitive, realistic—are not hard to discover. In fact there are two reasons. Firstly, these were the qualities expressed in the pastoral care and leadership of the Lord Jesus and his apostles. And, secondly, Tim Witmer himself exemplifies them. Our Lord said that the good shepherd knows his sheep and is prepared to lay down his life for the sheep. He spends time with them, gets to know them, and brings them to the Heavenly Father in prayer. And he does this because he "loves them to death." These are the qualities of the "shepherds after my heart" that God has promised to give to his people. When these qualities are combined with an understanding and wise application of Scripture, God's flock will be shepherded. We need this desperately today when so many are "like sheep without a shepherd." These pages have the potential to transform the way undershepherds together lead their flocks. Few things would bring its author—and his Shepherd—greater satisfaction and joy.

Sinclair B Ferguson
First Presbyterian Church
Columbia, S.C.

INTRODUCTION

"THERE IS A CRISIS in the church!" Books like this always begin by sounding an alarm. In this case it is a shepherding crisis, or should I say a failure to shepherd. There can be no better introduction to the subject than a "real-life" scenario (details changed):

> Cathy Williams, affectionately known to many as "Kate," was born on September 22, 1953. In 1986, Cathy became a member of Covenant Church on the basis of her profession of faith and remained a member until her death on July 14, 2005. The death of Cathy Williams became a watershed moment in the pastoral shepherding ministry of Covenant Church. Coming out of a rebellious and loose lifestyle, Cathy made a profession of faith and actively participated in the life of the church. But then she began to fall into her old sinful habits. She abandoned the church and no one knew where she was; or at least no one cared to find out. Her name, however, remained on the rolls of the church, but just as a name. Shortly before her death, God placed Cathy back on the doorstep of Covenant Church. Pastoral interaction with the dying Cathy was too brief to confirm how she stood before God. In a cloud of uncertainty, Cathy was memorialized. She will have to stand before the judgment seat to give account for her life, but before that same

throne the undershepherds of the flock at Covenant will have to give account for this one lost sheep.

How many Cathys are there in your church? What is the leadership of your church doing to care for these people? What view do your leaders hold of their identity as leaders and, therefore, what they are supposed to do? What is *your* view of the nature and function of leadership in the church? What is your *congregation's* view of the nature and function of leadership in the church?

The simple thesis of this book is, "The fundamental responsibility of church leaders is to shepherd God's flock." After all, the word "pastor" comes from the Latin word meaning "shepherd." However, as you will see, shepherding is not merely the responsibility of those who are called to be pastors but also of those who are called to be elders or its equivalent in our churches. In fact, you will see that "shepherding" is at the very heart of the biblical picture of leadership. Unfortunately, this emphasis is missing in many churches.

Some years ago I attended a series of meetings designed to encourage leaders in our denomination. One well-respected pastor conducted a seminar on leadership and began by introducing us to the most important biblical metaphors for leadership. As he moved through his list of biblical terms I kept waiting for him to mention the metaphor of "shepherd," expecting that it was certainly going to be next. However, it wasn't on his list at all! With the concept of shepherding so conspicuously absent from meetings such as this one, it should be no surprise that the ministry of shepherding leaders is conspicuously absent in many of our churches today.

Therefore, though this is not a book on church polity, it will challenge your thinking on the nature, function, and structure of leadership in your church. This is important because the failure to shepherd in our churches is the simple but dangerous result when church members and leaders fail to embrace this fundamental biblical model. For example, if the church leader is called to be a "shepherd," those chosen to serve will be different than if he is to be *merely* a "decision-maker." Are the elders or leadership team a "board of directors" making decisions, or is it a team of shepherds caring for the flock? The answer to this question will also have an impact on whether the primary qualification for your leadership team is corporate success and experience or a shepherd's heart. Obviously, they are not necessarily mutually exclusive, but what is the *fundamental* orientation of your leaders?

The failure to shepherd produces several symptoms, and we can observe at least one *micro* symptom and one *macro* symptom. The *micro* symptom can be seen in the closing verses of Matthew 9. As Jesus walked through the cities and villages of Galilee we are given the following description: "Seeing the people, He felt compassion for them, because they were distressed and dispirited like sheep without a shepherd" (Matt. 9:36). What Jesus observed among the people was described in terms that evoke frustration and discouragement: "distressed and dispirited." These words could well be used to describe the people in many of our churches today. The sheep are frustrated and discouraged because they are not receiving the care that they need and that the Lord requires that his shepherds provide. Many of them may be spiritually hungry or may have even begun to stray. Failure to shepherd, therefore, impacts church *health*.

This leads quite naturally to a *macro* problem when these discouraged sheep wander from church to church swelling the roles of some churches while other congregations shrivel away and die. This may explain the American phenomenon of the apparent success and vitality of some megachurches, which grow even though church membership and attendance continue to decline overall. Thus, there is an impact on church *growth*. If we understand this dynamic we will see that "a sheep retained is as valuable as a sheep gained."

How did we get into this predicament? There are many reasons for this development, but most fundamentally, either church leaders don't know that shepherding is what they are supposed to do, or they don't know how to do it. This book is designed to prove to you from the Bible that church leaders, specifically elders, are fundamentally undershepherds. Having proven that point, the book will then help you to implement an effective shepherding ministry in your church.

This subject came to my attention as I was doing my doctoral work at Reformed Theological Seminary in Orlando, Florida. Having been converted through the ministry of Campus Crusade for Christ and then involved in a church plant followed by an urban church revitalization project, I was deeply concerned about the subjects of evangelism and mission. After all, in both circumstances it was urgent that the church grow in number! As I reflected on my experience, though, I came to realize that in both settings, people were heading out the back doors nearly as quickly as they were coming in the front (or side) doors, and there came a point when numerical growth stopped. How was it possible that, though we were doing the same things to reach people and were moderately successful in bringing them into the church, overall it was as if we were "treading water": lots of activity but getting nowhere. How was this possible? This led me to do some reminiscing about my own spiritual pilgrimage. I, like so many baby boomers, grew up in the church, but when I left home for college, concern from my church ended. I never heard from anyone at the church, except my parents, of course. This is the reason that most baby boomers, for example, should not technically be characterized as "unchurched Harrys" *a la* Willow Creek's lexicon, but as "prechurched Petes." One study among baby boomers cited by Wade Roof claims that "two-thirds of all boomers reared in a religious tradition *dropped out* of their churches and synagogues during their teens or early twenties."[1] How did this happen? Apparently, the church leaders of the "builder" generation did not do a very good job in shepherding their children. The Roof study also made the startling observation that "dropping out of organized religion during the young adult years, at least for a transitory period in a person's life, is a deeply imbedded cultural problem in America."[2] Now another generation is at stake. The millennial generation (born between 1980 and 2000) is making its impact on the culture and the church. Will our churches fail them? If they or anyone else "drops out," will anyone notice? Will anyone respond and seek them with a shepherd's heart? Are we going to find more "Cathys?"

An important factor to keep in mind as a church leader is the matter of our accountability for the stewardship of leadership entrusted to us by the Lord. The writer of Hebrews tells us, "Obey your leaders and submit to them, for they are keeping watch over your souls, as those who will have to give an account" (Heb. 13:17). The motivation for the sheep to respect those in leadership is the clear realization that these leaders will have to give an account to the Lord one day for their flocks. This is among the "texts that terrify" as one of my seminary professors used to say. It should certainly motivate us to understand

1. Wade Clark Roof, *A Generation of Seekers* (New York: Harper Collins, 1993), 154.
2. Ibid., 56.

what the shepherding language of "keeping watch over your souls" means.

Therefore, this book is designed to be a practical guide 1) to convince you that shepherding provides a comprehensive framework for what you need to be doing as a church leader and 2) to provide a practical guide to help you start a shepherding ministry among your people, or to improve the one you already have. Though I am a professor at a theological seminary, this is not primarily an academic work, but I hope those studying (and teaching) in seminaries will find it to be valuable. I am a professor of *practical theology*, so my motivations are pastoral with the humble desire of helping you apply these principles in your ministry setting.

The following chapters will move from the biblical and historical foundations to practical application. The first section will convince you, I hope, that shepherding is something you should be concerned about, and the subsequent sections will move toward the "how to's" of what a shepherding plan should look like. At the heart of the "how to" section are the seven elements of an effective shepherding ministry. These "elements" are not "pick and choose." Each of them needs to be in place if your shepherding plan is to be effective. The concluding chapters will highlight some important implications of having a commitment to shepherd the flock as well as suggest some practical ways to implement a shepherding ministry.

For the sake of simplicity, I will refer to church leaders as "elders," reflecting what I believe to be the biblical model of leadership in the local church. If you do not have "elders" (though I hope that within these pages I can persuade you to employ the biblical terminology!), please "fill in the blanks" with the terminology used for the leadership team at your church.

This book would not have been possible without the congregation and officers of Crossroads Community Church (PCA), who not only model these principles but allowed me the time to put them into print. Crossroads' elders are truly shepherds! I am also grateful to the faculty and students at Westminster Theological Seminary (Philadelphia), who helped me to refine and clarify the principles you find here. This material has also been impacted by the scores of churches and hundreds of officers to whom I have had the joy of presenting it over the past ten years. It's great to know that there are so many who are eager to grow in their effectiveness as shepherds. My thanks also to Mr. and Mrs. Robert Herr who allowed me to spend some time on their *Nix Besser* (None Better!) sheep farm in Lancaster County, Pennsylvania. Their insights in caring for real sheep have helped me to appreciate the wisdom of God in applying the metaphor to his people. I am also grateful to Marvin Padgett, Aaron Gottier, and Eric Anest of P&R for shepherding me through the development of this work, and to Larry Sibley for compiling the Scripture index. Last, but not least, I thank the Lord for my dear wife, Barbara, without whose unconditional love and support this book would still be a dream.

My prayer is that your flock will not be like "sheep without a shepherd." Rather, may it be said of you as it was said of the shepherd-king, David, "So he shepherded them according to the integrity of his heart, and guided them with his skillful hands" (Ps. 78:72).

PART 1

BIBLICAL AND HISTORICAL FOUNDATIONS

While this book is designed to provide a very practical model for shepherding ministry, no church should embrace a ministry model that cannot demonstrate its biblical rationale. Though the Bible is not a detailed "book of church order," the Lord has provided clear principles designed to guide his church for its ongoing health and growth, particularly with regard to the nature and functions of church leaders. The concept of the leader as a shepherd is a theme with deep roots in God's written revelation with its foundations in the Old Testament and fulfillment in the New. Chapters one and two will provide the biblical background, and chapter three will give a brief overview of the theme through the subsequent history of the church. Before we embark on the "how to's" of the next section, chapter four will address the important biblical foundations of a shepherd's "right" to exercise the biblical leadership functions.

I

Not a New Idea: Old Testament Themes

The Lord as the Shepherd of His People

"The Lord is my shepherd, I shall not want." (Ps. 23:1 KJV)

THE BIBLICAL IMAGERY of the Lord as the shepherd of his people is plentiful and rich throughout the Bible.[1] It begins in Genesis where, as Jacob blessed his sons, he described the Lord as "the God who has been my shepherd all my life" (Gen. 48:15).

---

1. A more detailed exposition of the biblical theology of the shepherding metaphor can be seen in Timothy S. Laniak's book *Shepherds After My Own Heart* (Downers Grove, IL: InterVarsity, 2006).

Jacob declared in faith that behind his tumultuous and often rebellious life was a faithful, patient Shepherd who provided for him and guided him. It was his intent to see his children blessed by yielding to the covenant lovingkindness of the Lord. The sense of personal care and blessing in covenant with the Lord is captured by the most familiar of psalms, which begins with the affirmation, "The Lord is my shepherd, I shall not want" (Ps. 23:1 KJV). The Lord is the ultimate provider, protector, and guide for his sheep.

However, the relationship that God established was not merely with individuals, but corporately with his people. It is natural, therefore, that God's covenant people are described in terms of his "sheep" and "flock." The psalmist cries out, "Hear us, O Shepherd of Israel, you who lead Joseph like a flock" (Ps. 80:1 NIV). The psalmist rejoices in the faithfulness of God to his covenant people, "Come, let us bow down in worship, let us kneel before the Lord our Maker; for he is our God and we are the people of his pasture, the flock under his care" (Ps. 95:6–7 NIV).

The description of the Lord as shepherd of his flock is often found in a redemptive context. There are numerous references, for example, that relate the redemption of the people from bondage in Egypt to the Lord as shepherd. "You led your people like a flock by the hand of Moses and Aaron" (Ps. 77:20 NIV) reflects on the goodness of God in delivering his people through the Red Sea. The very next psalm recounts the destructive plagues poured out upon the Egyptians but then remembers that "he brought his people out like a flock; he led them like sheep through the desert" (Ps. 78:52 NIV). These accounts not only celebrate his protective care from the Egyptians but lay the foundation for the climactic redemptive deliverance yet to come.

The Lord's self-revelation as "shepherd" of his people is not merely a metaphor with which his people could clearly relate, but it is one that describes the comprehensive care that he provides for his people. Again, this is clearly seen in Psalm 23, where the Lord's care for his people leads to the superlative expression of gratitude and praise from his people, "I shall not want." Nothing is lacking in the care provided for the flock. Not only does he feed them, but he also leads them and protects them.

The reassurance of his faithfulness is given to them even when they are straying. Isaiah writes, "He tends his flock like a shepherd: He gathers the lambs in his arms and carries them close to his heart; he gently leads those that have young" (Isa. 40:11 NIV). When the work of shepherding is difficult, the commitment of the shepherd is truly revealed. Yet shepherding is a labor of love to the one who truly is a shepherd.

The shepherding metaphor is not only comprehensive with respect to the nature of the care received but also with respect to the extent. This is one important distinction between the metaphor of father and that of shepherd. Children grow up and become less dependent on their earthly fathers, though the relationship continues. Sheep, on the other hand, are *always* completely dependent on their shepherd. They never outgrow their need for the shepherd to care for them, feed them, lead them, and protect them. The shepherd cares for the newborn lambs and is still there when the sheep grow old and weak. Therefore, the imagery of shepherd-sheep captures the comprehensive sovereignty of the shepherd over the sheep and the need of the sheep to yield completely to his care. The good news is that the Lord uses his sovereign power for the well-being of his flock.

Shepherd-Leaders of Israel: Moses and David

If the Lord is the shepherd and the people are his flock, we should not be surprised that he uses shepherding imagery to refer to those he calls to lead and care for his flock. The care of the Lord for his people is to be reflected in those whom he calls to lead.

Two of the preeminent leaders of God's people in the Old Covenant, Moses and David, are described in this way. In addition to the reference from Psalm 77 in the previous section, Isaiah identifies Moses as a shepherd of Israel. "Then his people recalled the days of old, the days of Moses and his people—where is he who brought them through the sea, with the shepherd of his flock" (Isa. 63:11 NIV)? While the grammatical construction of the Hebrew text is difficult, E. J. Young definitively concludes that the "shepherd" is Moses: "On the one view it is God who delivered the people and with them the shepherd of His flock; on the other it is Moses who as the shepherd brought the people up from the Red Sea."[2] Moses was used by the Lord to lead God's covenant people, his flock, from bondage in Egypt.

David's leadership is also described in terms of shepherding. When the people of Israel rallied around him as their king, they reminded him that "the LORD said to you, 'You will shepherd my people Israel, and you will become their ruler'" (2 Sam. 5:2 NIV). In recounting the glory of David's rule, the psalmist writes that "David shepherded them with integrity of heart; with skillful hands he led them" (Ps. 78:72 NIV).

2. Edward J. Young, *The Book of Isaiah* (Grand Rapids: Eerdmans, 1972), 484.

In addition to these specific references to Moses and David as shepherd-leaders, there is a general reference to all of Israel's leaders as shepherds. In 2 Samuel 7, the Lord instructs Nathan to respond to David's desire to build a house for the Lord. In that context the Lord tells Nathan, "Wherever I have moved with all the Israelites, did I ever say to any of their rulers whom I commanded to shepherd my people Israel, 'Why have you not built me a house of cedar'" (2 Sam. 7:7 NIV)? The previous rulers are described as those "commanded to shepherd" the people.

Did you ever think about that fact that Moses and David were called from shepherding *real* flocks to shepherd the people of God? It was while tending his father-in-law's sheep that the Lord spoke to Moses from the burning bush, calling him to deliver the covenant people (Ex. 3:1ff). The Lord took Moses' humble shepherd's staff and transformed it into the symbol of God's call and through which his mighty deeds were accomplished that brought the people out of bondage. "You shall take in your hand this staff, with which you shall perform the signs" (Ex. 4:17). It was this staff that became a serpent in the presence of Pharaoh. It was through the staff that, in the Lord's power, the Nile was turned to blood, the dust was turned to gnats, the hail fell on Egypt, and the locusts came upon the land. It was when this staff was lifted up that the waters of the Red Sea parted and God's people passed through safely. When Moses raised it again the waters crashed down on Pharaoh's soldiers and chariots. It was with the staff that Moses struck the rock in Horeb and the water flowed in quantities sufficient to satisfy the thirst of his people in the desert.

> Then the LORD said to Moses, "Pass before the people and take with you some of the elders of Israel; and take in your hand your staff

15

with which you struck the Nile, and go. "Behold, I will stand before you there on the rock at Horeb; and you shall strike the rock, and water will come out of it, that the people may drink." And Moses did so in the sight of the elders of Israel. (Ex. 17:5–6)

It was this staff that Moses held high on the mountain while Joshua and the Israelites fought in the valley and won their first post-exodus victory over the Amalekites. As long as the staff was held high, Israel prevailed, but as Moses' arms grew weary and the staff came down, the Amalekites prevailed.

So Moses said to Joshua, "Choose men for us and go out, fight against Amalek. Tomorrow I will station myself on the top of the hill with the staff of God in my hand." Joshua did as Moses told him, and fought against Amalek; and Moses, Aaron, and Hur went up to the top of the hill. So it came about when Moses held his hand up, that Israel prevailed, and when he let his hand down, Amalek prevailed. (Ex. 17:9–11)

Aaron and Hur helped him hold the staff high, and the Amalekites were defeated. No wonder it was referred to as the "staff of God" (Ex. 4:20). Moses was the human "undershepherd," but there was no doubt that the "staff of God" revealed that it was the Lord who was protecting the people, providing for the people, and guiding the people.

David was another leader whom God called right from the sheepfolds. The psalmist writes, "He chose David his servant and took him from the sheep pens; from tending the sheep he brought him to be the shepherd of his people Jacob, of Israel his inheritance" (Ps. 78:70–71 NIV). In each case, David and Moses were prepared for service in the Lord's flock by working with real sheep. When David was persuading Saul to allow him to take on the Philistine champion, Goliath, he used his experience in protecting the sheep as the foundation of his argument.

> Then Saul said to David, "You are not able to go against this Philistine to fight with him; for you are but a youth while he has been a warrior from his youth." But David said to Saul, "Your servant was tending his father's sheep. When a lion or a bear came and took a lamb from the flock, I went out after him and attacked him, and rescued it from his mouth; and when he rose up against me, I seized him by his beard and struck him and killed him. Your servant has killed both the lion and the bear; and this uncircumcised Philistine will be like one of them, since he has taunted the armies of the living God." (1 Sam. 17:33–36)

David found courage to face Goliath in the strength the Lord had given him to protect his father's flocks from the lions and bears. Lessons learned in the sheepfold about feeding, leading, and protecting flocks would be essential in ministering to God's people. The Lord's purpose would be fulfilled in preserving a remnant of his people in his land from whom would issue the promised Messiah, the ultimate Shepherd of God's people. Moses, the prototypical prophet, and David, the prototypical king, are both described as shepherds. In providing shepherding care for the people of God, they were reflecting the shepherding care of the covenant Lord.

The Problem with Human Shepherds

Moses

The ultimate inadequacy of human shepherds is also clearly revealed in the Old Testament. The power of God was shown

17

mightily through Moses' humble staff, which became the "staff of God." However, misuse of that same staff became his stumbling block when Israel faced the need for water again in the desert: "Take the rod; and you and your brother Aaron assemble the congregation and speak to the rock before their eyes, that it may yield its water. You shall thus bring forth water for them out of the rock and let the congregation and their beasts drink" (Num. 20:8).

However, instead of speaking to the rock as the Lord commanded, Moses struck the rock with the staff. This act of insubordination and disrespect led to Moses' disqualification from entering the land. "But the LORD said to Moses and Aaron, 'Because you have not believed Me, to treat Me as holy in the sight of the sons of Israel, therefore you shall not bring this assembly into the land which I have given them'" (Num. 20:12). There was to be no confusion over who was the shepherd of Israel. In the end there was no doubt that it was the Lord who brought the people into the land of promise.

David

King David also fell short when he abused his power as shepherd-king of Israel; first in his adultery with Bathsheba and then in the subsequent conspiracy in the murder of her husband, Uriah. The king should have been deployed with his army for the sake of the protection of God's people. Instead, he remained behind and abused the sheep. Nathan the prophet was sent by the Lord to confront David with his sin. Remember the parable that he told?

Then the LORD sent Nathan to David. And he came to him and said, "There were two men in one city, the one rich and the other poor. The rich man had a great many flocks and herds. But the poor man had nothing except one little ewe lamb which he bought and nourished; and it grew up together with him and his children. It would eat of his bread and drink of his cup and lie in his bosom, and was like a daughter to him. Now a traveler came to the rich man, and he was unwilling to take from his own flock or his own herd, to prepare for the wayfarer who had come to him; rather he took the poor man's ewe lamb and prepared it for the man who had come to him." (2 Sam. 12:1–4)

The story Nathan told would have resonated with David as he understood the malice of this selfish shepherd. His own shepherd's instinct based on his experience evoked a response of righteous indignation.

Then David's anger burned greatly against the man, and he said to Nathan, "As the LORD lives, surely the man who has done this deserves to die. He must make restitution for the lamb fourfold, because he did this thing and had no compassion." (2 Sam. 12:5–6)

When Nathan told him, "You are the man!" David immediately understood the evil he had committed and repented.

David would never think of abusing sheep in that way, but he had committed an even greater transgression by abusing God's sheep. As Moses' failure as Israel's shepherd resulted in consequences for himself and the people, so with King David. Moses, the one who bore the staff of God, had failed and would not enter the Promised Land. David, who wore the crown of the "shepherd-king," would see the death of the infant son born from the illicit union with Bathsheba. His sin had an even

19

greater impact, as Nathan prophesied: "Now therefore, the sword shall never depart from your house, because you have despised Me and have taken the wife of Uriah the Hittite to be your wife" (2 Sam. 12:10). Though the Lord called men to shepherd his flock, it became more and more apparent with every succeeding generation that the people needed to look to the Lord as their shepherd and king and that the undershepherds themselves needed to be vigilant in following the Lord. Unfortunately, the frailty of human shepherds continued to be a major theme in Israel's history.

Ezekiel 34

Moses and David demonstrated their fallibility as shepherds, but Israel's shepherds as a whole incurred the chastisement of the Lord in an episode that should be sobering to all who are called to positions of leadership among God's people.

Ezekiel prophesied among God's people during a very difficult time in Israel's history. He had been carried away into exile in Babylon along with the unfaithful Israelites. His ministry among them was manifold, including "to impress upon the exiles the fact that the calamity had come because of their own sinfulness."[3]

The thirty-fourth chapter of Ezekiel's prophecy represents detailed charges against the undershepherds of Israel, who should have been caring for God's flock. These would have been the elders of the nation whose unfaithfulness was largely responsible for the circumstances in which the people found themselves. The Lord held them accountable for their failure to

3. Edward J. Young, *An Introduction to the Old Testament* (Grand Rapids: Eerdmans, 1989), 244.

shepherd the flock. The chapter contains three major sections. The first section (34:1–10) includes the detailed indictment against the shepherds. The appropriate use of the shepherding metaphor is front and center throughout the chapter. What are the charges?

They fed *themselves* rather than the flock (verse 2); they failed to strengthen the sickly, heal the diseased, bind up the broken, and seek the lost (verse 4). The result for the people was that they were scattered, literally to a foreign land, and became food for every beast of the field (verse 5). As you can see, they failed to fulfill the most basic functions of shepherds: to feed, lead, and protect the sheep. Instead, the sheep were starved, lost, and the prey of wild animals. Even worse, those who were supposed to feed and protect God's flock were actually feeding upon the sheep themselves: "You eat the fat and clothe yourselves with the wool, you slaughter the fat sheep without feeding the flock" (Ezek. 34:3).

Verse 4 also speaks of the manner of their approach, "with force and severity you have dominated them." Laniak comments that this terminology of brutality is only used elsewhere in the Old Testament where it describes slavery in Egypt.[4] The concluding verses (7–10) of the first section declare the Lord's opposition to the shepherds and their removal so that they can do no more damage to God's flock.

> Therefore, you shepherds, hear the word of the LORD: "As I live," declares the Lord GOD, "surely because My flock has become a prey, My flock has even become food for all the beasts of the field for lack of a shepherd, and My shepherds did not search for My flock, but rather the shepherds fed themselves and did not feed

4. Laniak, *Shepherds After My Own Heart*, 153.

My flock; therefore, you shepherds, hear the word of the LORD: 'Thus says the Lord GOD, "Behold, I am against the shepherds, and I will demand My sheep from them and make them cease from feeding sheep. So the shepherds will not feed themselves anymore, but I will deliver My flock from their mouth, so that they will not be food for them."'" (Ezek. 34:7–10)

In the second section of the chapter (verses 11–22) God promises shepherding care for his people. Though they have been mistreated, God has not forgotten them.

> For thus says the Lord GOD, "Behold, I Myself will search for My sheep and seek them out. As a shepherd cares for his herd in the day when he is among his scattered sheep, so I will care for My sheep and will deliver them from all the places to which they were scattered on a cloudy and gloomy day." (Ezek. 34:11–12)

Every failure of the undershepherds will be met by the Lord. He himself will seek the lost sheep, care for them, feed them, and protect them. He will lead them to rest, bind up the broken, and strengthen the sick. He also reiterates that he will hold those to account who have abused his flock.

One of the consequences of the failure to shepherd is that others will step in to fill the void. The strong will assert themselves and bully the weaker sheep.

> Therefore, thus says the Lord GOD to them, "Behold, I, even I, will judge between the fat sheep and the lean sheep. Because you push with side and with shoulder, and thrust at all the weak with your horns until you have scattered them abroad." (Ezek. 34:20–21)

Faithful shepherds protect their flocks not only from harmful outside influences but from the self-serving among the sheep. Many congregations have experienced the intimidation of bullies within their midst when leaders fail to take responsibility to shepherd the flock. It is often the strong-willed, outspoken, highly opinionated folk who fill the void. There will *always* be leaders—the issue is whether they are the leaders called and gifted by God to shepherd his flock or those who push themselves forward so that they can push others around.

The third section of the chapter (verses 23–31) looks forward to the coming of the perfect shepherd. Would there ever be one upon whom the Father could depend to give faithful care to his flock? Ezekiel looks forward with prophetic vision to the shepherd who is to come. "Then I will set over them one shepherd, My servant David, and he will feed them; he will feed them himself and be their shepherd" (Ezek. 34:23).

The times in which Ezekiel wrote were long after the days of the shepherd-king, David. However, there was another shepherd-king to come, and his faithfulness would eclipse not only that of the unfaithful shepherds during Ezekiel's time, but that of David, Israel's revered shepherd-king. In fact, the one of whom Ezekiel speaks is the promised one to come who will have an everlasting reign on David's throne (see 2 Sam. 7:12). The one who is to come will not merely be a king but a shepherd-king. This concluding section once again sounds the notes of the shepherding metaphor but now in an eschatological key. There is yet to come a new covenant, a "covenant of peace," the blessings of which will be brought to his people by the Messianic shepherd-king. He will be the ultimate provider, deliverer, and guide.

The chapter concludes with two important statements. Verse 30 reminds the people of the personal covenantal relationship that God has established with them. "'Then they will know that I, the Lord their God, am with them, and that they, the house of Israel, are My people,' declares the Lord God." The covenant with Israel was established that they might be his people and that he would be their God, so they can be assured of his lovingkindness and comprehensive shepherding care.

As verse 30 reminds the people about the uniqueness of the relationship between the Lord and his people, the final verse of this remarkable chapter reminds the people that they must not forget that *he* is God. "'As for you, My sheep, the sheep of My pasture, you are men, and I am your God,' declares the Lord God" (Ezek. 34:31).

It is always incumbent upon the people of God to remember that he is not only their shepherd, but that he is the Lord God. Yet the sheep were not the only ones who needed to hear this message. The undershepherds of Israel failed to remember that they themselves were the Lord's sheep, resulting in the scattering of the flock and their own condemnation. These words continue to serve as a vivid reminder to those who would lead his flock of their accountability to the Lord for the manner in which they care for his sheep.

The Shepherd to Come

As we have just seen, the closing words of Ezekiel 34 point forward to *the* Good Shepherd who will have none of the shortcomings of sinful human shepherds. However, Ezekiel wasn't the only prophet who used the shepherding metaphor to describe the coming Messiah. In a passage that closely reflects the structure of Ezekiel 34, Jeremiah 23 gives a more condensed version of the condemnation of the false shepherds.

> "Woe to the shepherds who are destroying and scattering the sheep of My pasture!" declares the LORD. Therefore thus says the LORD God of Israel concerning the shepherds who are tending My people: "You have scattered My flock and driven them away, and have not attended to them; behold, I am about to attend to you for the evil of your deeds," declares the LORD. (Jer. 23:1–2)

As with Ezekiel, the hopelessness of the situation was not to prevail. Jeremiah also provides a promise of the coming Davidic shepherd-king:

> "Behold the days are coming," declares the Lord, "when I will raise up for David a righteous Branch; and He will reign as king and act wisely and do justice in the land. In His days Judah will be saved, and Israel will dwell securely; and this is His name by which He will be called, 'The Lord our righteousness.'" (Jer. 23:5–6)

The imagery of a well-protected flock is pictured as the prophet reflects on the current insecurity of Israel in Babylonian captivity. It is the "righteous Branch" from the lineage of David who will bring about deliverance for his people.

Later in redemptive history, Micah picks up this theme. Most are familiar with Micah's prophecy about the place of the coming Messiah's birth. However, many don't recall Micah's actual description of the One who is to come. After identifying Bethlehem Ephrathah as the birthplace of the "ruler over Israel," Micah describes him as the one who "will stand and shepherd his flock in the strength of the LORD, in the majesty of the name of the LORD his God. And they will live securely, for then his greatness will reach to the ends of the earth" (Mic. 5:2, 4 NIV). The gospel of Matthew quotes these words in the context of the search of the Magi for the one "who has been born king of the Jews" (Matt. 2:2). This promise was fulfilled in the coming of Jesus, the Shepherd-King. He would succeed in faithfully shepherding God's flock where all others had failed.

For Further Reflection

1. Why is the metaphor of shepherd appropriate for the relationship between God and his people?
2. Compare and contrast the imagery of shepherd and father as descriptions of the Lord's relationship with his people.
3. Why is the metaphor of shepherd appropriate for those who would lead the people of God?
4. Using the chart on the next page follow and identify the parallels between the Lord's indictment of Israel's faithless elders, his commitment to shepherd them, and the shepherd to come. Discuss implications for your ministry as shepherds of his flock today.

Ezekiel 34:1–10 The Lord's Indictment of Faithless Elders	Ezekiel 34:11–22 The Lord As Israel's Shepherd	Ezekiel 34:23–31 The Shepherd to Come

2

FULFILLMENT: THE GOOD SHEPHERD AND THE APOSTOLIC IMPERATIVE

"Therefore, I exhort the elders among you, as your fellow elder and witness of the sufferings of Christ, and a partaker also of the glory that is to be revealed, shepherd the flock of God among you, exercising oversight not under compulsion, but voluntarily, according to the will of God; and not for sordid gain, but with eagerness; nor yet as lording it over those allotted to your charge, but proving to be examples to the flock." (1 Peter 5:1–3)

IN THE GOSPEL OF JOHN, Jesus declares, "I am the good shepherd" (John 10:11, 14). These words were rich with meaning to his original listeners. In addition to listeners' familiarity with the vocation of the shepherd in their own day, they would have

29

heard Jesus' identification with the Lord, Israel's shepherd. Jesus, then, declares himself to be the Shepherd-King who had been prophesied by Ezekiel and Jeremiah. Where human shepherds had failed, Jesus as God incarnate would not.

He uses shepherding imagery to describe his relationship with the sheep. "I am the good shepherd; I know my sheep and my sheep know me" (John 10:14 NIV). But who are his sheep? Jesus makes it very clear that the identifying mark of his sheep is that they hear his voice. "Hearing" is not merely auditory perception but a spiritual understanding that responds in faith. "My sheep listen to my voice; I know them, and they follow me. I give them eternal life, and they shall never perish; no one can snatch them out of my hand" (John 10:27–28 NIV). The sheep are drawn by the effectual call of the Good Shepherd into the safety of his fold. The identifying mark of his sheep is that they hear his voice and follow him by faith. On the contrary, those who are not his sheep do not believe. The identification of the sheep as sheep is determined ultimately in the sovereign plan of God.

Jesus as the consummate shepherd provides for the comprehensive care of his sheep. He knows that it is not merely sufficient for them to be fed with real bread—their need is far deeper. This spiritual hunger and thirst can only be met through faith in him. "Jesus said to them, 'I am the bread of life; he who comes to Me will not hunger, and he who believes in Me will never thirst'" (John 6:35). His sheep will find their sustenance in him and his word as they walk with him.

Jesus not only provides for his sheep, but he calls them to follow wherever he lovingly leads them. A mark of true disciples is that they follow their shepherd. This theme is sounded in the call of the very first apostles. He said to them, "Follow Me, and I will make you fishers of men" (Matt. 4:19). Jesus also emphasized that "if anyone wishes to come after Me, he must deny himself, and take up his cross daily and follow Me" (Luke 9:23). Jesus goes on ahead to prepare a place for his sheep that where he is, there they may follow.

> "Do not let your heart be troubled; believe in God, believe also in Me. In My Father's house are many dwelling places; if it were not so, I would have told you; for I go to prepare a place for you. If I go and prepare a place for you, I will come again and receive you to Myself, that where I am, there you may be also. And you know the way where I am going." Thomas said to Him, "Lord, we do not know where You are going, how do we know the way?" Jesus said to him, "I am the way, and the truth, and the life; no one comes to the Father but through Me." (John 14:2–6)

Earlier in John 10 Jesus uses familiar shepherding imagery as he refers to himself as "the door of the sheep" (John 10:7). By using this language he defines the exclusive means of entrance into the flock. "I am the door; if anyone enters through Me, he will be saved and will go in and out and will find pasture" (John 10:9). Only those who enter through him will enjoy the comprehensive care that only he can provide.

All of these promises, however, are based on a unique element of his care for the sheep. Jesus describes himself as the one who "lays down His life for the sheep" (John 10:11). While the work of the shepherd could be dangerous at times in warding off wild animals, giving up his life "must have been a fairly rare occurrence among Palestinian shepherds."[1] Ordinarily, the shepherd's calling was not to die for the sheep but to live for the sheep. Jesus'

---

1. Leon Morris, *The Gospel of John* (Grand Rapids: Eerdmans, 1971), 509.

charge was unique, however, as he came to provide protection from the ultimate eschatological danger of condemnation for sin through giving his life as the substitutionary atonement for the transgressions of his flock. He laid down his life and was able to "take it up again" (John 10:18), his resurrection from the dead being the exclamation point on his finished work on behalf of the sheep. The comprehensiveness of his care extends through eternity and, therefore, his sheep are absolutely secure.

The security of the sheep is seen in that "no one will snatch them out of My hand" (John 10:28). The word describing the action of would-be thieves ("snatch"; *arpadzein* in Greek) means to "seize" or "take by force." Any potential thieves and robbers must deal with Jesus, who has already conquered sin and death on behalf of his sheep. There is no chance that they can succeed. If this promise were not enough, Jesus reminds his listeners that to be secure in him is to be secure in the Father as well. Not only can no one snatch them out of his hand, but "no one is able to snatch them out of the Father's hand" (John 10:29). To be secure in Christ is to be secure in the Father, and that is to be secure completely and secure forever. Now that is security! Jesus is the promised Good Shepherd, and through him the sheep "will dwell in the house of the Lord forever."

More Shepherds Needed

Jesus' concern for the ongoing care of his sheep was clearly seen as he walked through the cities and villages of Galilee. "Seeing the people, He felt compassion for them, because they were distressed and dispirited like sheep without a shepherd" (Matt. 9:36). He not only saw their condition and their need, but he saw the cause of the problem. As Ezekiel and Jeremiah had connected the weakened condition of the Israelites with the failure of the elders to shepherd the flock, Jesus also pointed to the absence of proper shepherds. "It is not simply human need that moves Jesus, but *their predicament as a flock not properly led.*"[2] His compassionate response was twofold. First, he commanded his disciples to "beseech the Lord of the harvest to send out workers into His harvest" (Matt. 9:38). Second, his compassion led to action. He immediately authorized and sent his disciples to "the lost sheep of the house of Israel" (Matt. 10:6). His mission was to become their commission. Jesus had every intention of providing shepherding care for his sheep, even in his absence. The apostles were to be the foundation of the perpetual ministry that Jesus intended for his flock.

The Apostolic Imperative

Exactly how would Jesus extend his shepherding care among his people after his resurrection and ascension? With the advance of his kingdom the shepherding metaphor does not retreat but continues to be at the forefront of Christian leadership. After all, it was in the context of the condemnation of the false shepherds of Israel and the promise of the Davidic shepherd that the Lord promised, "'I will also raise up shepherds over them and they will tend them; and they will not be afraid any longer, nor be terrified, nor will any be missing,' declares the LORD" (Jer. 23:4). Could Jeremiah be looking forward with prophetic vision to the

2. Timothy S. Laniak, *Shepherds After My Own Heart* (Downers Grove, IL: Inter-Varsity, 2006), 185.

calling of faithful shepherds who would carry on the mission of Jesus the Good Shepherd in the days of the New Covenant? The Lord would continue to provide care for his people through Spirit-filled, -gifted, and -called undershepherds.

Peter

An examination of the apostolic record in the New Testament reveals that the leader's function as shepherd is at the very heart of his calling. Peter's words to church leaders in the fifth chapter of his first letter are instructive:

> Therefore, I exhort the elders among you, as your fellow elder and witness of the sufferings of Christ, and a partaker also of the glory that is to be revealed, *shepherd the flock* of God among you, exercising oversight not under compulsion, but voluntarily, according to the will of God; and not for sordid gain, but with eagerness; nor yet as lording it over those allotted to your charge, but proving to be examples to the flock. And when the Chief Shepherd appears, you will receive the unfading crown of glory. (1 Peter 5:1–4)

First of all, Peter refers to himself as a "fellow elder" (Greek, *sumpresbuteros*) demonstrating continuity in the authority of the office: "Though he was an apostle, he yet knew that authority was by no means delegated to him over his colleagues, but that on the contrary he was joined with the rest in the participation of the same office."[3] There is not merely continuity in authority but also solidarity in the essential service of the office as well. That service is described in the urgent call to "shepherd the flock

3. John Calvin, *Calvin's Commentaries: Commentaries on the Catholic Epistles* (Grand Rapids: Baker, 1984), 144.

of God among you." The verb "shepherd" (Greek, *poimaino*) is in the emphatic position and the imperative mood, indicating that shepherding the flock is the essential work of the elder according to Peter. "There is no word in the whole round of primitive ecclesiastical phraseology which is more frequently used to express the relation of office-bearer than 'to shepherd.'"[4]

This should be no surprise after an examination of a cathartic event in Peter's life recorded in the twenty-first chapter of John's gospel. Commentators generally agree that this event "is meant to show us Peter as completely restored to his position of leadership."[5] After his threefold denial of the Lord, he returned to fishing in Galilee. It was on the shores of the Sea of Galilee that the risen Savior appeared to the disciples for the third time since his resurrection. Jesus asked Peter, "Do you love me?" not once, but three times, corresponding to his three denials. While commentators dispute the significance of the change in Greek words for "love" in the exchange (*agapao* and *phileo*), of great interest in our understanding of the importance of shepherding is the three-fold charge Jesus issued in response to Peter's affirmation of affection and loyalty.

After each reaffirmation of Peter's loyalty, Jesus responded with a command for him to heed. Have you ever thought about this? While there were any number of aspects of the work of leadership that Jesus could have stressed, each time he used terminology that brought Peter's attention to the imperative of caring for the flock. In the first and third instances, Jesus used the verb to "feed" (Greek *boskein*). In the second instance, he used the verb to "shepherd" (Greek *poimainein*). Trench observes

---

4. Thomas M. Lindsay, *The Church and the Ministry in the Early Centuries* (Minneapolis: James Family Publishers, 1977), 162.

5. Leon Morris, *The Gospel According to John* (Grand Rapids: Eerdmans, 1971), 875.

that "*boskein* . . . is simply 'to feed,' but *poimainein* involves much more; the whole office of the shepherd, the guiding, guarding, folding of the flocks, as well as finding nourishment for it."[6] Morris adds, "Most people see the variation as no more than stylistic."[7] In *all three* imperatives the risen Christ calls Peter to the work of caring for the flock. The response of Jesus to Peter's affirmations of love and affection *could* have included three *different* charges. For example, he could have said "preach the Gospel," "make disciples," or "love one another" or any other combination of imperatives. Instead, when he was in the process of restoring Peter, he responded in each case with imagery related to shepherding the flock: "Tend My lambs," "Shepherd My sheep," and "Tend My sheep" (John 21:15–17).

Returning to the fifth chapter of Peter's first epistle, with the echoes of his Lord's words in mind, Peter charged those elders who were to continue in leadership to "shepherd the flock of God." This is the essential work of the elders of the church. Peter also spoke to their "hearts" to remind them of how they were to go about this work.

Peter's description of elders serves as a stark contrast to the false shepherds described in Ezekiel 34. The false shepherds of Israel were condemned because they fed themselves and clothed themselves with the wool, but Peter tells leaders that they are to shepherd the flock "not for sordid gain, but with eagerness" (1 Peter 5:2). Ezekiel's shepherds dominated the flock "with force and severity," but Peter reminds the elders that they are not to shepherd "as lording it over those allotted to your charge, but proving to be examples to the flock" (1 Peter 5:3).

6. Richard C. Trench, *Synonyms of the New Testament* (London: Kegan, Paul, Trench, Trubner, and Company, 1894), 85.

7. Morris, *John*, 874.

Another parallel between Ezekiel's words and Peter's words is that shepherds are accountable to the Lord for how they lead. Peter describes Jesus as the "Chief Shepherd" (Greek, *archipoimen*) of the sheep (5:4), and Selwyn notes that the word "underlines its relationship to those who have pastoral charge in the Christian ministry. In relation to them Christ is the *chief* shepherd, set over them yet sharing their function."[8] In this context, however, Peter doesn't set threats of judgment before them but rather the promise of the "unfading crown of glory." If the faithless shepherds of Ezekiel's day could expect judgment, how much more should faithful shepherds anticipate reward for fulfilling their calling from their Chief Shepherd? While the noun form of the Greek word for "shepherd" (*poimen*) is used only once in reference to church leadership (Eph. 4:11), the verb form is found numerous times as a description of the work of the elder. "Shepherd" or "undershepherd," therefore, are both appropriate terms to apply to elders who, together with all who preceded them, are ultimately accountable to the Chief Shepherd for their charge to care for the flock entrusted to them.

Paul

The apostle Paul also connects the work of shepherding with leadership, particularly with the office of elder. The definitive passage is found in the twentieth chapter of the book of Acts, where Luke records Paul's farewell to his beloved elders of the church in Ephesus. Beginning in the seventeenth verse, Paul defends his ministry among the Ephesians as one of faithfulness to the ministry of the gospel, "solemnly testifying to both Jews

---

8. Edward G. Selwyn, *The First Epistle of Peter* (Grand Rapids: Baker, 1981), 231–32.

and Greeks of repentance toward God and faith in our Lord Jesus Christ" (Acts 20:21). For several verses he reviews his ministry among them, reminding them not only of his message but of his method among them. His address concludes with a solemn charge to the Ephesian elders: "Keep watch over yourselves and all the flock of which the Holy Spirit has made you overseers. Be shepherds of the church of God, which he bought with his own blood" (Acts 20:28 NIV). When called to summarize the work of the elders in these final moving words, he returns to the imagery of shepherding. The elders are to be vigilant in "watching over" (*prosecho*) not only themselves but also the believers at Ephesus. It is noteworthy that they are described as overseers (*episkopous*). Calvin observed that "according to the use of the Scripture, bishops (*episkopoi*) differ nothing from elders (*presbuteroi*)."[9] F. F. Bruce agrees with Calvin's assessment:

> There was in apostolic times no distinction between elders (presbyters) and bishops such as we find from the second century onwards: the leaders of the Ephesian church are indiscriminately described as elders, bishops, (i.e. superintendents) and shepherds (or pastors).[10]

Lightfoot concurs, writing that "it has been shown that in the apostolic writings the two are only different designations of the same office."[11] The distinction between the terms elder and overseer (bishop) is described by Bruce in the fact that "the term

9. John Calvin, *Calvin's Commentaries*, ed. Henry Beveridge (Grand Rapids: Baker, 1984), 19:255.

10. F. F. Bruce, *Commentary on the Book of Acts* (Grand Rapids: Eerdmans, 1970), 415.

11. J. B. Lightfoot, *Saint Paul's Epistle to the Philippians* (London: MacMillan and Company, 1913), 193.

elder has mainly Jewish antecedents, while bishop has mainly Greek antecedents."[12] The synonymous nature of the two terms is confirmed by their usage together here in Acts 20.[13] The action to which both terms point and to which elders and overseers must be committed is "to shepherd the church of God."

In summary, both Peter and Paul stressed the centrality of the work of shepherding when addressing the elders of the churches. In Peter's words we detect continuity with the words of reinstatement issued by his risen Lord, representing the necessity for the perpetuation of the work of shepherding throughout the ages. In the finality of Paul's words to the Ephesian elders he clearly emphasizes that their labors must be as shepherds of God's people.

Implications for Church Structure

The biblical material makes it clear that the heart of the work of the elder is to shepherd the flock. Having said this, it is important to note some important implications for church structure.

The plurality of leadership. Together with the picture of leaders as shepherds, the New Testament describes teams of elders working together within particular churches. As Paul and Barnabas planted churches they "appointed elders for them in each church and, with prayer and fasting, committed them to the Lord, in whom they had put their trust" (Acts 14:23 NIV). This implies a

12. Bruce, *Acts*, 416n56.

13. In chapter 3 we will see how these terms began to be applied to different offices to the detriment of the ongoing shepherding care of the church.

plurality of elders working *together* within each of the churches. When Paul was on his way to Jerusalem, he "sent to Ephesus for the elders of the church" (Acts 20:17 NIV). Paul continued this apostolic pattern, instructing Titus to "appoint elders in every town, as I directed you" (Titus 1:5 NIV), after which he outlined the qualifications Titus should look for in such men. John Murray summarized Paul's teaching quite clearly: "Titus was enjoined to ordain *elders* in every city. He was not instructed to ordain an elder or bishop in every city. Paul called to Miletus the elders of the church and charged them, as a plurality, to shepherd the flock of God."[14]

This pattern is not limited to the Pauline material. James urged those who were sick to "call the elders of the church to pray over him and anoint him with oil in the name of the Lord" (James 5:14). This text assumes a relationship between the sick person and a particular group of elders who are the elders of the church, that is, the sick person's church. "One notices that in James it is not just any older person who is called, but officials, the elders of the church, which in this case is surely the *local congregation*"[15] (emphasis added).

In Peter's words "to the elders among you" he admonishes them to shepherd God's flock "that is under your care." The point is that each congregation had a number of men who were charged *together* with the responsibility of shepherding the flock. In your congregation, it is not only wise but biblical to develop a team of elders who are gifted and called to shepherd the flock. Of course, Presbyterian church government is designed to reflect this biblical model, and many other churches have seen the wisdom of the biblical pattern and sought to conform to it. For example, many

14. John Murray, *Collected Writings* (Carlisle, PA: Banner of Truth, 1977), 2:345.
15. Peter Davids, *Commentary on James* (Grand Rapids: Eerdmans, 1982), 193.

independent and Baptist church leaders, whose commitments are rooted in congregational church government, have seen the importance of returning to this biblical model of church leadership. Baptist leader Mark Dever has noticed the trend:

> As late as the early twentieth century, Baptist publications were referring to leaders by the title of *elder*; but as the twentieth century wore on, the idea seemed to vanish, until today it has become very unusual for a Baptist church to have elders. Today, though, there is a growing trend to go back to this biblical office—and for good reason. It was needed in New Testament times and it is needed now."[16]

The casual observer can see the wisdom of the plurality of elders in a local church. That is, if it is understood that the elders are not merely called to be decision-makers but to be involved personally with the sheep.

The parity of church leadership: elders and pastors. "Parity" is a word that is used essentially as a synonym for "equality." In discussions of the eldership it merely means that, with respect to authority and accountability, elders are on the same "level" with one another. As usual, John Murray gets right to the point: "There is not the slightest evidence in the New Testament that among the elders here was any hierarchy; the elders exercise government in unison, and on a parity with one another."[17]

This doesn't mean that they have the exact same responsibilities. For example, the New Testament teaches that there are elders

16. Mark Dever, *Nine Marks of a Healthy Church* (Wheaton, IL: Crossway, 2000), 215.

17. Murray, *Collected Writings*, 2:346.

whose gifts lead them to spend significant time in preaching and teaching the Word. Paul speaks of those who are "pastor-teachers" (see Eph. 4:11), those who are not only shepherds but who focus on teaching the Scriptures. In fact, these "teaching elders" might gain their livelihood from their teaching ministry. Paul speaks to this situation in his first letter to Timothy.

> The elders who rule well are to be considered worthy of double honor, especially those who work hard at preaching and teaching. For the Scripture says, "You shall not muzzle the ox while he is threshing," and "The laborer is worthy of his wages." (1 Tim. 5:17–18)

Paul was not only making the point that there are those whose gifts and calling require them to "work hard at preaching and teaching," but that their efforts may be acknowledged in the form of monetary compensation. This, together with the references Paul offers in support,[18] is the biblical precedent for compensating those leaders in the church who forego other means of gainful employment to carry out their calling to study, preach, and teach the Scriptures among the flock. There are obvious examples of people who have chosen to forego this rightful compensation for one reason or another. Paul himself served as the model "tentmaker" for those who by choice or necessity have not exercised their right to be compensated for their ministry of the Word. The text also implies that those who "rule well" might also be compensated for their labors.

One of the practical outcomes of the identification of those who give themselves to preaching and teaching is that these individuals have often become viewed as *primus inter pares*—first

18. See Deut. 25:4; Lev. 19:13.

among equals. This may have practical benefits in terms of providing initiative and direction in the local church. However, we must not lose sight of the fact that the biblical picture of leadership is "team" leadership. All elders, including teaching elders (pastors), are called to shepherd the flock, but not all elders have the gift of teaching, though they should be apt to teach.

The point of this discussion isn't who should or should not be compensated for their ministry but to focus on the fact that all who are called to be elders are called to the sheep-intensive work of shepherding. They are called to exercise their leadership *together* for the benefit of the flock. In many cases, probably because he is the one receiving a paycheck, the work of shepherding the people of God has fallen exclusively to the teaching elder or pastor. He is the one who visits the people. He is the one to whom people look for counsel. He is the one who is viewed as the "shepherd" of the local congregation. However, given what we have seen about the centrality of the work of shepherding to those who are called to be elders, this makes no sense! How is the teaching elder supposed to have the time to give careful attention to the preaching and teaching ministry of the Word if he is charged with shepherding the *entire* flock as well? No, the biblical picture is of a shared responsibility among all of the elders for shepherding the flock. If anything, the teaching elder should have *less* responsibility in some shepherding functions so as to have sufficient time to carry out his responsibilities in preaching and teaching the flock.

We look at the plethora of reports that come out year after year about pastoral burnout and the alarming number of clergy leaving their churches or leaving the ministry altogether. Might not one of the contributing factors be that they are not receiving the help they need in shepherding the flock prescribed in the Scriptures? Not only will our churches be healthier, but the work of the pastor will also be more manageable if all elders take seriously the work that Christ has called them to do in sharing the responsibility to shepherd the flock.

For Further Reflection

Review Acts 20:17–38.

1. What were the elements of Paul's ministry to the people of Ephesus?
2. What are the terms used to describe the leaders of the church?
3. To what fundamental imperative does Paul's appeal build?

Review 1 Peter 5:1–4.

4. How does this text reveal the continuity and discontinuity between Peter the apostle and the elders to whom he wrote?
5. What imperative is central to his charge to elders?
6. Compare 1 Peter 5:1–4 with Ezekiel 34. Identify the stark contrasts between the behavior of the elders in Ezekiel 34 and the heart of an elder as described by Peter.
7. Do the elders of your church think of themselves primarily as shepherds or as a board of directors? How do they share the responsibilities of shepherding the flock?
8. Do the members of the church perceive their leaders as shepherds?
9. Does your form of church government reflect the biblical model of shepherding elders?

3

LOST AND FOUND: WHERE
DID ALL THE SHEPHERDS GO?

A Brief Historical Survey

IF THE BIBLICAL material is clear that elders are to be shepherds and that the office of elder has been established by the Lord to care for the flock in a partnership of plurality and parity, why is there so much confusion about this in the church today? One of the answers to this enigma is that through the centuries the church has followed a circuitous route away from the New Testament pattern and back. The biblical understanding of the nature and work of the office of elder as shepherd has been "lost and found," and sometimes lost again! This brief historical overview will help you see this journey and perhaps help you understand how your church came to its current practice. It cannot be exhaustive but will focus on key individuals and their impact on these issues.

Before the Reformation

In the previous chapter, ample biblical evidence was presented that in the apostolic era the primary task for elders was shepherding and that the different terms for elder (*presbuteros*, *episkopos*) are synonymous for the same office. In the inspired writings of both Paul and Peter it is clear that the work of the elder is shepherding and that the work is to be shared among a plurality of elders in a particular location. Paul sent for the "elders [*presbuteroi*] of the church" in Ephesus (Acts 20:17). Peter's words were penned to "the elders [*presbuteroi*] among you" (1 Peter 5:1).

Outside the canon of Scripture, there is additional first century confirmation of the continuation of the plurality of leadership in the early church. Clement's Epistle to the Corinthians (c. AD 96) represents this continuing practice. The occasion of the letter was rebellion by a few against the elders of the church. (Evidently, the church at Corinth continued its feisty ways long after Paul's appeals for love and unity.) First of all, Clement argues for the validity of the offices of "bishops" and "deacons" in the local church.

> So, preaching in country and city, they [apostles] appointed their firstfruits, having tested them by the Spirit, to be bishops and deacons, of those who should believe. And this was no novelty, for long ago it had been written concerning bishops and deacons. For the Scripture says, "I will establish their bishops in righteousness and their deacons in faith."[1]

1. W. K. Lowther Clarke, ed., *The First Epistle of Clement to the Corinthians* (London: Society for Promoting Christian Knowledge, 1937), 72.

He notes that the apostles appointed bishops and deacons (plural) with the implication that these were appointed wherever churches were established. Throughout his letter, Clement uses "bishop" and "presbyter" interchangeably. While there are those who disagree, this quotation confirms the ordinary and perpetual nature of the offices of bishop (presbyter) and deacon.

Clement goes on to praise those who were deposed and to question the actions of those responsible.

> Blessed are the presbyters who have gone before in the way, who came to a fruitful and perfect end; for they need have no fear lest anyone depose them from their assigned place. For we see that you have removed certain men of good behaviour from a ministry blamelessly and honorably fulfilled.[2]

As the letter continues, he becomes even more pointed in his criticism and refers to the plurality of elders in the church:

> It is disgraceful, brethren, very disgraceful, and unworthy of Christian conduct, that of the stable and ancient Church of the Corinthians, thanks to one or two persons, it should be reported that it revolts against its presbyters.[3]

He then suggests a course of action to those who have caused the trouble.

> Who among you is noble? Who is compassionate? Who is filled with confident love? Let him say: "If on my account there are sedition and strife and schisms, I will depart, I will go wherever you wish and will do what is commanded by the

2. Ibid., 74.
3. Ibid., 76.

community; only let the flock of Christ be at peace with the appointed presbyters.[4]

Nearly two thousand years later, this problem sounds all too familiar! For the purposes of this chapter, you can see that it was the plurality of elders who were responsible to shepherd the flocks of believers in the Roman empire at the end of the first century. Consider church historian Thomas Lindsay's outlook:

> These statements . . . prove to us that before the close of the first century bodies of presbyters existed as ruling colleges in Christian congregations over a great part of the Roman Empire. The Epistle of Clement proves this for the Roman Church. The First Epistle of Peter proves it for Pontus, Galatia, Cappadocia, Asia, and Bithynia.
>
> The Apocalypse confirms the proof for Ephesus, Smyrna, Pergamus, Thyatira, Sardis, Philadelphia, and Laodicea. The Acts of the Apostles adds its confirmation for Ephesus and Jerusalem.[5]

The work of the elders in the first century was shepherding the local flocks of believers in their respective locations.

However, in the second century a gradual shift began that was to have dramatic ramifications on the nature of the organization and ministry of the church. Instead of the local church being overseen by a plurality of elders, with the assistance of the deacons, the seeds of hierarchical practice were planted. There arose a single person who became the "bishop" or "pastor" of a single church and then a group of churches.

4. Ibid., 79.
5. Thomas Lindsay, *The Church and the Ministry in the Early Centuries* (New York: G. Doran, 1902), 163.

The change made consisted in placing at the head of this college of rulers [elders] one man, who was commonly called either the pastor or the bishop, the latter name being the more usual, and apparently the technical designation. The ministry of each congregation or local church instead of being, as it had been, two-fold—of elders and deacons—became three-fold—of pastor or bishop, elders and deacons.[6]

However, it wasn't until the third century that the seed planted in the second century came to full bloom as authority increasingly shifted from the plurality of the elders to one bishop.

Rather than seeing authority in the church and the care for the flock as the responsibility of all of the elders, a single bishop took the preeminent position. This was advanced largely through the work of Cyprian (c. 200–258). With specific respect to the effect of this change upon care for the flock, Lindsay provides this summary of the impact of Cyprian's perspective:

> The bishop had entire charge of the discipline of the congregation. . . . It was his duty to instruct the people about what the discipline of the Church required, and to promote their growth in holiness. . . . In all this the elders and deacons might assist, but always under the control of the bishop. To him and to him alone belonged the right of "binding and loosing"—a right which had been given, he maintained, to St. Peter, and then to the other apostles, and which now belonged to the bishops . . . [7]

Together with this change was a drift to a sacerdotal focus in ministry, drawing a direct parallel between the Levitical

6. Ibid., 170.
7. Ibid., 303.

priesthood and the office of bishop in the New Covenant. Once again, Cyprian was a key catalyst.

> Cyprian . . . applies all the privileges, duties, and responsibilities of the Aaronic priesthood to the officers of the Christian church and constantly calls them *sacerdotes* and *sacerdotium*. He may therefore be called the proper father of the sacerdotal conception of the Christian ministry as a mediating agency between God and the people. During the third century it became customary to apply the term "priest" directly and exclusively to the Christian ministers, especially the bishops.[8]

This served not only to distance the bishop from the laity but to elevate the bishop over the other offices in the church as well.

The focus of the ministry narrowed to the growing list of sacraments and the worthiness or unworthiness of members to participate. While there was some responsibility shared, it was quite clear that "no restoration of sinners was possible until the bishop had heard their confession, had approved of their signs of sorrow, or until he along with the presbyters and deacons, had placed his hands on their head in token of forgiveness."[9] As the church continued to move away from the parity of the elders in overseeing the flock, the hierarchy of the church gained more and more authority. Abuse of authority also grew to the point where no longer did the officers exist to serve the flock, but the flock was held increasingly captive by superstition and fear. Strauch summarizes the result: "Due to the 'deceitful light of human authorities,' which replaced the New Testament teaching on eldership, the Christian doctrine of eldership was lost

8. Philip Schaff, *History of the Christian Church* (Grand Rapids: Eerdmans, 1910), 2:126–27.

9. Lindsay, *The Church and the Ministry*, 304.

for nearly fourteen centuries."[10] For more than a millennium, "pastoral care" became identified with the hearing of confessions by an anonymous confessor who would prescribe ready-made penance to the dutiful sinner.

The New Testament teaching not only on eldership but on even more fundamental doctrines of the faith had been eclipsed in the shadows of the increasing focus on the human traditions of the church. It would take nothing less than a return to the Bible to bring the church back to the foundational truths as well as to those truths which provided for the proper care of the people of God through active shepherd-elders. This return would come with the Reformation.

The Reformation

It was as early as John Wycliffe (1329–84), the "morning star of the Reformation," that the recognition of the biblical warrant for the two-office view reappeared.

One thing I boldly assert, that in the primitive church, or in the time of the Apostle Paul, two orders of clergy were thought sufficient, viz. *priest* and *deacon*; and I do also say that in the time of Paul . . . a priest and a bishop were one and the same; for, in those times, the distinct orders of Pope, Cardinals, Patriarchs, Archbishops, Bishops, arch-Deacons, officials, and deans, were not invented.[11]

10. Alexander Strauch, *Biblical Eldership* (Littleton, CO: Lewis and Roth, 1995), 11.
11. Cited in Peter A. Lillback, "The Reformers' Rediscovery of Presbyterian Polity," in *Pressing Toward the Mark: Essays Commemorating the Fifty Years of the Orthodox Presbyterian Church*, ed. Charles Dennison and Richard Gamble

With the arrival of the Reformation in full force, not only were the foundational, Scriptural doctrines of the faith redis- covered, but progress was to be made in the biblical structure of the church.

While the original Reformation battles were fought largely over the fundamental issues of doctrine, attention was eventu- ally paid to what constituted true biblical order in the offices in the church. John Calvin (1509–64) clearly saw that the bibli- cal sword cut through the multilayered hierarchy of the day to reveal the simplicity of the divine pattern. "In calling those who preside over Churches by appellations of bishops, elders, pas- tors, and ministers, without any distinction, I have followed the usage of Scripture, which applies all these terms to express the same meaning."[12]

However, he did not see these terms as synonymous with what we would call the "ruling elder" but with the office of "pastor" of the local congregation. Appreciation for the "lay" leader who would assist in shepherding the flock would become apparent later in his pastoral ministry.

He was deeply concerned for the care of the people of Geneva and urged the city council to clearly define the parishes of the city for this purpose. Unfortunately, they delayed in doing so. Calvin complained in a letter to Bullinger that this led the people to view their ministers merely as preachers rather than pastors.[13] When he returned to the city in 1541 the council complied with his request.

(Philadelphia: Committee for the Historian of the Orthodox Presbyterian Church, 1986), 67.

12. John Calvin, *The Institutes of the Christian Religion*, trans. Ford Lewis Battles (Philadelphia: Westminster Press, 1960), 2:324.

13. Amy Nelson Burnett, "A Tale of Three Churches," in *Calvin and the Company of Pastors*, ed. Daniel Foxgrover (Grand Rapids: CRC Product Services, 2004), 111.

He outlined his understanding of four offices[14] for the ongoing work of the ministry in Geneva. They were teachers (or doctors), pastors, elders, and deacons. In the *Institutes* he provides a description of the work of the elder or "governor":

> "Governors" I apprehend to have been men of advanced years, selected from the people to unite with the bishops in giving admonitions and exercising discipline. For no other interpretation can be given that injunction, "He that ruleth, let him do it with diligence." Therefore, from the beginning, every Church has had its senate or council, composed of pious, grave, and holy men, who were invested with that jurisdiction in the correction of vices, of which we shall soon treat. Now, that this regulation was not of a single age, experience itself demonstrates.[15]

Those given responsibility for the "care of the poor" were the deacons. The "Governors" or "ruling elders" were another category of elder in distinction from the pastors. The increasing importance of the "ruling elder" can be seen in his later exposition of 1 Timothy 5:17:

> We may learn from this, that there were at that time two kinds of elders; for all were not ordained to teach. The words plainly mean, that there were some who "ruled well" and honourably, but who did not hold the office of teachers. And, indeed, there were chosen among the people men of worth and of good character, who, united with the pastors in a common council, and authority, administered the discipline of the Church, and were a kind of censors for the correction of morals. Ambrose complains that this custom had gone into disuse, through the

14. See *Ecclesiastical Ordinances of 1541*.
15. Calvin, *Institutes*, 324–25.

carelessness, or rather through the pride, of the doctors [teachers] who wish to possess undivided power.[16]

The work of the ruling elders largely consisted in overseeing the respective congregations of the Geneva community:

> The duties of the elders were "to keep watch over every man's life, to admonish amiably those whom they see leading a disorderly life, and where necessary, to report to the assembly which will be deputized to make fraternal correction."[17]

This order of the offices was reflected later in the French Confession of Faith (c. 1559) authored by Calvin and his pupil, De Chandieu:

> As to the true Church, we believe that it should be governed according to the order established by our Lord Jesus Christ. That there should be pastors, overseers, and deacons, so that true doctrine may have its course, that errors may be corrected and suppressed, and the poor and all who are in affliction may be helped in their necessities.[18]

This succinct summary provides each office with a brief description of the functions of the offices as well. Pastors were responsible to see that "true doctrine may have its course," overseers were to assure that "errors may be corrected and suppressed," and deacons were to help the poor and needy.

16. John Calvin, *Calvin's Commentaries*, vol. 21, ed. and trans. William Pringle (Grand Rapids: Baker, 1984), 138–39.

17. Richard A. Gamble, "Switzerland: Triumph and Decline," in *John Calvin: His Influence in the Western World*, ed. W. Stanford Reid (Grand Rapids: Zondervan, 1982), 57.

18. Philip Schaff, *The Creeds of Christendom* (New York: Harper and Brothers, 1877), 3:376–77.

Calvin's interest in shepherding the flock was noteworthy:

Jean Daniel Benoit, the expert on Calvin's work in the cure of souls, states boldly that the Geneva Reformer was more pastor than theologian, that, to be exact, he was a theologian in order to be a better pastor. In his whole reforming work he was a shepherd of souls.[19]

In summarizing Calvin's influence, Strauch comments that Calvin

... decried the loss of the church eldership and promoted its restoration. The sixteenth century efforts, however, were only partially successful because the Reformers could not break free from the hardened soil of long-standing, clerical traditions.[20]

However, even in the Reformed churches, the transition from monarchical episcopacy to the biblical parity of eldership in caring for the flock took time to develop in principle and practice. It can be argued that Calvin and the continental reformers were more attentive to challenge the complicated layers of prelacy in the Roman church than they were to sort out the role of "governors" and ruling elders. However, one can see that his convictions about the importance of the ruling elder grew over time.

Calvin's views reverberated to the British Isles, where his most famous student, John Knox (1514–72), would introduce reform to Scotland. This was particularly the case with Knox's view of lay elders. Knox followed Calvin in the view that the minister of the Word was supported by ruling elders in caring for the flock. In his account of the establishment of church leadership in Edinburgh:

19. John T. McNeill, *A History of the Cure of Souls* (New York: Harper and Row, 1951), 198.
20. Strauch, *Biblical Eldership*, 11.

And becaus the Spirit of God will never suffer his awne to be idle and voyde of all religioun, men began to exercise thamesekfis in reading of the Scriptures secreitly within thair awne houses; and varietie of persones culd not be keipt in gud obedience and honest fame, without Oversiers, Elders and Deacons: And so begane that small flocke to put thameselfis in sick ordour, as if Christ Jesus had planely triumphed in the middes of thame by the power of his Evangell. And thay did elect sum to occupie the supreame place of exhortation and reading [the Scriptures], som to be Elderis abd helpers unto thame, for the oversight of the flocke: And some to be Deacones for the collectioun of almes to be distributed to the poore of thair awne bodie.

Of this small begyninf is that Ordour, quihilk now God of his grit mercie hes gevin unto us publictlie within this Realme. Of the principalls of thame that were knowne to be men of gude conversatioun and honest fame in the privy Kirk, were chosen Elders and Deacones to reull with the Minister in the publicke Kirk.[21]

The work of the elder was described in both the First and Second Book of Discipline:

Thair office is, als weill severallie as conjuntlie, to watche diligentlie upone the floc committit unto thair charge, bayth publicklie and privatlie, that no corruptioun of religioun or maneris enter thairin.[22]

It continues to distinguish the functions of the elder from the pastor and doctor:

21. John Knox, *Works*, ed. David Laing, (Edinburgh: The Wodrow Society, 1861), 2:151.

22. *The Second Book of Discipline*, ed. James Kirk (Edinburgh: The Saint Andrew Press, 1980), 193.

> As the pastouris and doctouris sould be diligent in teacheing and sowing the seid of the word, so the eldaris[23] sould be cairfull in seiking the fruict of the same in the peple.[24]

Though the elders did not necessarily have gifts of teaching, there was no doubt that they were to share the responsibility for the care of the flock in the kirk:

> The authority of the elders was high in the Scottish Kirk. In John Knox's liturgy there was provision for a weekly (Thursday) meeting of ministers and elders chiefly for mutual criticism, but also for consideration of the faults of the members. The elder's office was redefined in the Second Book of Discipline (adopted 1581) where elders were to assist in the examination of communicants and in visiting the sick, as well as to give "private admonition" and to join with pastors and "doctors" in "establishing good order and execution of discipline."[25]

The ministers and elders met together *weekly* to consider the health and discipline of the flock.

Puritan England

While the idea of monarchical episcopacy saw its demise in Scotland under the leadership of Knox and his immediate

---

23. In the early documents of the Reformed Scottish church, elders were also known as *governouris* and *Seniors*. The term *governouris* is a direct connection to Calvin's terminology and *Seniors* represents the idea of maturity in years implied in the Greek *presbyteros*.

24. *Second Book*, 193.

25. McNeill, *History of the Cure of Souls*, 249.

successors, the struggle continued in England through the Puritans. Again, though their primary concern was to clearly articulate the Reformed faith, the Westminster Assembly (1643–49) sought to address matters of church order. There is little in the Westminster Larger or Shorter Catechisms concerning the office or functions of church leaders. There are only vague references to those we have come to know as lay ruling elders. There are references to "the minister" as the one who can rightly administer the sacraments of the New Covenant (Westminster Larger Catechism, Question 176). This is an explicit reference to the "teaching elder" in distinction from the ruling elder.

It is in chapter 30 of the Westminster Confession on "Church Censures" that there is a more general reference to the officers of the church and their function:

1. The Lord Jesus, as King and Head of his Church, hath therein appointed a government, *in the hand of Church officers*, distinct from the civil magistrate.

2. *To these officers the keys of the kingdom of heaven are committed*; by virtue whereof, they have power, respectively, to retain and remit sins; to shut that kingdom against the impenitent, both by the Word and censures; and to open it unto penitent sinners, by the ministry of the Gospel; and by absolution from censures, as occasion shall require.

3. Church censures are necessary, for the reclaiming and gaining of offending brethren, for deterring of others from the like offences, for purging out of that leaven which might infect the whole lump, for vindicating the honour of Christ, and the holy profession of the Gospel, and for preventing the wrath of God, which might justly fall upon the Church, if they should suffer under His Covenant, and the seals

thereof, to be profaned by notorious and obstinate offenders.[26] (emphasis added)

Paragraph one refers to "Church officers," and it is very encouraging that the accompanying biblical proof-texts offered in support[27] include general references to "elders" and "leaders." Paragraph two recognizes the perpetual authority of the keys extended to the officers of the church, citing Matthew 16:19 and 18:17–18. Paragraph three makes an explicit reference to the believer's covenant faithfulness as a basis for taking disciplinary action. The implication is that the officers of the church are responsible to keep watch over the flock, " . . . preventing the wrath of God, which might justly fall upon the Church, if they should suffer His covenant . . ."

Among the documents produced by the Westminster Assembly is "A Directory for Church-Government, for Church Censures, and Ordination of Ministers." The following summary is found under the heading "Of the Officers of a particular Congregation": "For Officers in a single Congregation, there ought to be one at the least, both to labour in the Word and Doctrine, and to Rule. It is also requisite that there should be others to join in Government."[28] A few sentences later, the following guidelines are given for the ruling elders' involvement in the oversight of a particular congregation: "Where there are many ruling officers in a particular congregation, let some of them more especially attend the inspection of one part, some of another, as may be

26. The Westminster Confession of Faith (Glasgow: Free Presbyterian Publications, 1994), 119–20.

27. Acts 20:17–18; Heb. 13:7, 17.

28. *The Form of Presbyterial Church Government* (repr., New York: Robert Lenox Kennedy, 1880), 57–58.

most convenient; and let them at fit times visit the several families for their spiritual good."[29] These words represent an important development in parity of the elders of the church in caring for the flock. A subsequent paragraph speaks of the partnership of "pastors and other ruling officers" in the exercise of discipline in a particular congregation.

It is noteworthy, however, that there is no order for the ordination of "ruling elders," only for the "minister of the Word." While there is occasional reference to ordination as "a solemn setting apart of a person unto some public church office," the context is clear that the focus of the document's teaching on ordination is the one who is referred to as the "minister of the Word, a minister for a particular congregation, and preaching presbyters."

In summary, the Westminster Assembly articulated the existence of the office of ruling elder in its statements about "church officers" and "church-governors," and it contends that these officers are, together with the "minister of the Word," responsible for the oversight and discipline of the church." However, "parity" with the "minister of the Word" was an expression that did not enter into the assembly's vocabulary. There was still progress to be made toward the biblical ideal of recognizing ruling elders who actively shared the responsibility to shepherd the flock.

In Puritan England, and perhaps in the western church since the Reformation, there has been no more exemplary model of pastoral care than that presented and practiced by Richard Baxter (1615–91). It is no surprise, in light of what has been seen above, that the touchstone for his classic work, *The Reformed Pastor*, was the charge to "shepherd the flock" found in Acts 20:28. In commenting on this text, Baxter said,

---

29. Cited by Wayne R. Spear, "The Westminster Assembly's Directory of Church Government," in *Pressing Toward the Mark*, 90.

"*A little flock*" does not here signify the whole church of Christ, but that particular church of which those elders had charge. "*Overseers*," that is, persons appointed by Christ to teach and guide those churches, or that particular church in the way of salvation. The same persons who before are called elders of the church of Ephesus are here called overseers, or bishops. "*to feed the church of God*"—by some rendering barely "*to feed*," but by others, "*to rule*." But it ought not to be confined to either. For it comprehends both, or the whole of the pastoral work.[30]

Even though he hints at the parity of eldership in this quote, it is obvious that the focus of his exhortation is to the "pastor" as *the* shepherd of each congregation. In a subsequent section in which he outlines the presuppositions of his work there is no doubt where he places the overwhelming responsibility for the oversight of the flock:

It is here implied that every flock should have their own pastor (or more than one), and that every pastor should have his own flock. As every troop or company in a regiment must have their own captain, and every soldier must know his own commander and colors, so it is the will of God that every church should have their own pastors, and that all of Christ's disciples should know their own teachers that are over them in the Lord. The church of Christ consists of particular churches, guided by their own overseers. And every Christian must be a member of one of these churches. . . . Though a minister is an officer in the church of Christ, yet he is in a special manner the overseer of that particular church which is committed to his charge. From this relationship of pastor and flock arise all the duties which we mutually owe to each other.[31]

30. Richard Baxter, *The Reformed Pastor* (1656; repr., Grand Rapids: Sovereign Grace Publications, 1971), 1.

31. Richard Baxter, *The Reformed Pastor* (1656; repr., Carlisle, PA: Banner of Truth, 1997), 88.

Baxter did not see the ruling elder as a key partner in the work of shepherding the flock. This is further indicated by his suggestion that if a minister was overwhelmed with the size of his flock that he hire "one or two assistants"[32] out of his own salary to help in the visitation of the flock. One is left to wonder how remarkable the impact would have been if Baxter had engaged the biblical office of lay ruling elder in the care of the flock of Kidderminster.

Of great encouragement in Baxter is his focus on taking a proactive and preventive approach to congregational care through regular visitation and catechizing of the families of the church. But it even took some time for him to commit to the work:

> I wonder at myself, how I was kept from so clear and excellent a duty. But the case was with me, as I suppose it is with others. I was long convinced of it, but my apprehensions of the difficulties were too great, and my apprehensions of the duty were too small and so I was long hindered from the performance of it. I imagined the people would scorn it, and none but a few, who had least need, would submit to it, and I thought my strength would never go through with it, having such great burdens on me before; and thus I long delayed it which I beseech the Lord of mercy to forgive. Whereas, upon trial I find the difficulties almost nothing (save only through my extraordinary bodily weakness) to that which I imagined; and I find the benefits and comforts of the work proved to be such, that I would not wish I had forborne it, for all the riches in the world.[33]

His words of admonition to be engaged in the caring discipline of the flock are also very challenging:

32. Ibid., 93.
33. Ibid., 43.

My second request to the ministers in these kingdoms is that they would at last, without any more delay, unanimously set themselves to the practice of those parts of Church discipline which are unquestionably necessary, and part of their work. It is a sad case, that good men should settle themselves so long in the constant neglect of so great a duty. The common cry is, "Our people are not ready for it; they will not bear it." But is not the fact rather that you will not bear the trouble and hatred which it will occasion? If indeed, you proclaim our churches incapable of the order and government of Christ, what do you do, but give up the cause to them that withdraw from us, and encourage men to look out for better societies, where that discipline may be had?[34]

Baxter's concern for the care of Christ's flock and his commitment to carry it out among the people is an example for any Reformed pastor. However, his care of the flock would have been enhanced by engaging those identified by the reformers as "governor" and by Calvin as one of two kinds of elders.

Scottish Presbyterianism

In the wake of the great impact of John Knox's foundational work, it was the Scottish expression of Presbyterianism where the model of the engagement of all the elders in the care of the flock would continue to be developed. Even this took some time inasmuch as a primary concern of the day was the larger argument for Presbyterianism versus Episcopalianism. A good example of the Scottish viewpoint is churchman James Bannerman (1807–68):

34. Ibid., 46–47.

The power of bearing rule and exercising government and discipline in the Church, is undeniably a lower exercise of ministerial authority than the power to preach the Gospel and administer the seals of the covenant of grace. And yet, by admission of all parties, presbyters are vested with this highest kind of power as their distinctive function,—a circumstance that renders it very difficult to believe that they are excluded from the lower power of ruling in the Church . . . [35]

The argument against hierarchical authority found in "the bishop" over and above "the presbyter" was at the heart of the controversy. He appeals to the synonymous uses of *presbuteros* (elder) and *episkopos* (overseer, bishop).

It is not difficult to recognize the reason for the use of the two terms, *presbuteros* and *episkopos*, as applicable to the same undivided office. The first of these *presbuteros*, was the title appropriated to the office of elder in the Jewish synagogue. . . . The second of these *episkopos* was a word in general use among the Greeks to denote any kind of overseer. . . . But that these words were but different titles of the same official personage, is abundantly proved by a variety of passages in the New Testament. The proof indeed is so strong as to now be acknowledged to be conclusive as to the point by the most candid of the Episcopalian controversialists. [36]

Again, though the point was being powerfully made in favor of the biblical view of the terminology, there was still more progress needed in making use of those who, together with

35. James Bannerman, *The Church of Christ* (1869; repr., Carlisle, PA: Banner of Truth, 1974), 2:291.
36. Ibid., 2:274.

the ministers, shared the "power of bearing rule and exercising government and discipline in the church."There were two additional Scotsmen whose examples are helpful to examine; one a teaching elder (Thomas Chalmers) and one a ruling elder (David Dickson).

Thomas Chalmers

Thomas Chalmers (1780–1847) truly had the heart of a shepherd. At that time it was not uncommon for those who shepherded rural congregations to visit their families annually: "It is the acknowledged duty and in rural districts the general practice of clergymen of the Established Church of Scotland to make an annual visitation of their parishes, when every house is entered and the general condition of each family as to education and church attendance is ascertained."[37]

When Chalmers became pastor of the Tron church in Glasgow he understood that personal shepherding ministry was not merely something for the rural population but for the city as well: "There was nothing in any town population so essentially different from a rural one as to render the ministrations of a devoted clergyman less efficacious in the one case than in the other."[38] Therefore, he set out to visit every family in his parish personally. "Its population was not exactly known, but it was believed to contain somewhere between eleven and twelve thousand souls. To visit every family of such a population within a year or two was a Herculean task, yet Dr. Chalmers resolved to accomplish it."[39]

37. William Hanna, ed., *Memoirs of the Life and Writings of Thomas Chalmers* (New York: Harper and Brothers, 1850), 2:118.
38. Ibid., 2:118–19.
39. Ibid., 2:119.

Needless to say, the visits were very brief, surprisingly allowing no time even for a prayer. On one occasion a dear old widow pleaded for a prayer to which Chalmers replied, "If I were to pray in every house I enter, it would take me ten years to get through the work."[40] His visits consisted of a series of brief but pointed questions as to the state of church attendance and education in the family.

Early in his ministry at the Tron he realized that his success would require the active involvement of his elders. This was not going to be an easy transition for many of them. "Some of the elders of the Tron Church were excellent men, but their chief duty was to stand at the plate, receive the free-will offerings of the congregation as they entered, and distribute them to the poor by a monthly allowance."[41] Under Chalmers's leadership, they were going to do more than "stand at the plate." In order to accomplish the "Herculean" task of caring for the people, the city was divided into parishes, each having at least one elder and one deacon. He developed the shepherding skills of his elders by taking them along when he visited people in their district.

Here is a picture of Chalmers on visitation with an elder:

"Well," he said, looking kindly over the shoulder upon his elder, who, scarcely able to keep pace with him was toiling up a long and weary stair, "Well, what do you think of this kind of visiting?" Engrossed with the toils of the ascent, the elder announced that he had not been thinking much about it. "Oh! I know quite well," said Dr. Chalmers, "that if you were to speak your mind, you would say that we are putting the butter very thinly upon the bread."[42]

40. Ibid.
41. Ibid., 2:130.
42. Ibid., 2:120.

The last comment about "thinly" buttered bread was undoubtedly a reference to the brevity of the visits and the vast numbers of parishioners that were being seen. Chalmers was determined to engage these undershepherds in their biblical ministry to the people. He was encouraged as newly ordained elders joined in the work. On the occasion of the ordination of new elders on December 20, 1816, his charge included the following words:

> I am well aware how widely the practice of our generation has diverged from the practice of our ancestors—how, within the limits of our Establishment, the lay office-bearers of the Church are fast renouncing the whole work of ministering from house to house in prayer, and in exhortation, and in the dispensation of spiritual comfort and advice among the sick, or the disconsolate, or the dying. . . . I shall therefore only say that I know of nothing which would give me greater satisfaction than to see a connection of this kind established between my elders and the population of those districts which are respectively assigned to them. . . . [43]

His journal is filled with accounts of the visitation of the people with his elders.

> *Tuesday.* - Met Mr. John Brown, elder, and took him and Mr. Montgomery to a visitation in the proportion [district] of the latter. Went through [visited] 230 people, and drank tea at Mr. Brown's . . . . [44]

It is quite amazing that they had the energy or the time for tea after such a whirlwind schedule!

43. Ibid., 2:505.
44. Ibid., 2:180.

Chalmers had great vision for ministering to all of the needs of all of the people in the parishes he served. He brought about dramatic reforms in education and ministry to the poor throughout the city.[45] The elders and deacons of the church were key partners in shepherding, and this continued as he moved from the Tron to St. John's parish:

> The parish of St. John's was divided into twenty-five districts, called proportions, each embracing from sixty to one hundred families. Reviving the ancient order of deacons, which in Scottish Presbyterian practice had long fallen into disuse, Dr. Chalmers appointed over each of these districts an elder and a deacon; the spiritual interests of his proportion being committed to the former, and its temporal interests to the latter.[46]

The deacons became active partners in caring for the needs of the poor in each "proportion." There were regular meetings to consider the requests that would come to them on a weekly basis. He truly understood that the offices of elder and deacon represent the comprehensive care that Christ provides for his flock.

David Dickson

The perspective of the ruling elder can be seen in Chalmers's contemporary, David Dickson (1821–85). He served as a ruling elder in the Free New North Church in Edinburgh for more than thirty years. He promoted not only the dignity of the office but also a practical approach to the involvement of the

45. Chalmers's comprehensive attention to education, health, and poverty in Glasgow became known as the "parochial" system.

46. Hanna, *Memoirs*, 2:293.

elders in shepherding the flock: "I have a deep conviction that, though the scriptural standing of the ruling eldership has been always maintained and defended by Presbyterian churches, it has never been worked out in practice so as to do the good it might do."[47]

"Working it out in practice" is just what he proceeded to do. He proposed "districts" for which each elder was responsible. He presented models for visitation of families, visitation of the sick, and guidelines for discipline. He also saw the importance of overseeing a member's participation in worship. The ruling elder "will find it useful to know where his people sit in church."[48] A unique focus in his work was his encouragement to elders to see that the members of the flock were engaged in the work of the ministry: "What a change would appear on the Church and the world if each professing Christian were doing something— something for Christ—even though it were a very little! Might not wilderness soon be turned into a fruitful field?"[49] This caring, "proprietary" attitude toward the flock was more characteristic of Scottish Presbyterianism than anywhere else.

Elders in America

When Presbyterianism spread to America, the Scottish church made a profound mark. "After the Restoration ... Presbyterianism lost its vitality in England, but through force of example and by immigration, the Scottish church in later years became a very

47. David Dickson, *The Elder and His Work* (repr., Dallas: Presbyterian Heritage Publications, 1990), 2.
48. Ibid., 15.
49. Ibid., 59.

powerful influence in America."[50] Would the Scottish emphasis on the importance of the shepherding elder be perpetuated in the American church?

Samuel Miller (1769–1860) was a good example of the efforts to represent the biblical perspective in the New World. He served as a pastor in New York City and later taught at Princeton Theological Seminary for thirty-five years. Noteworthy are his words on the authority of the ruling elder:

> The ruling elder, no less than the teaching elder (or pastor), is to be considered as acting under the authority of Christ in all that he rightfully does. If the office of which we speak was appointed in the apostolic church by infinite wisdom—if it is an ordinance of Jesus Christ, just as much as that of the minister of the gospel—then the former, equally with the latter, is Christ's officer. He has a right to speak and act in his name; and though elected by the members of the church . . . yet he is not to be considered as deriving his authority to rule from them, any more than he who "labours in the word and doctrine" derives his authority to preach and administer other ordinances from the people who make choice of him as their teacher and guide.[51]

Miller also outlined the practical duties of overseeing the flock:

> But besides those duties which pertain to ruling elders, with the pastor, in their collective capacity as a judicatory of the church, there are others which are incumbent on them at all

50. Sydney E. Ahlstrom, *A Religious History of the American People* (Garden City, NY: Doubleday, 1975), 330–31.

51. Samuel Miller, *The Ruling Elder* (1831; repr., Dallas: Presbyterian Heritage Publications, 1994), 12.

times, in the intervals of their judicial meetings, and by the due discharge of which they may be constantly edifying the body of Christ. It is their duty to have an eye of inspection and care over all the members of the congregation; and, for thus purpose, to cultivate a universal and intimate acquaintance, as far as may be, with every family in the flock of which they are made "overseers."[52]

Miller saw the need for elders to be concerned with the flock "at all times," not merely when meeting as the "judicatory" of the church. He made it clear that the ideal was for the elders to be engaged in the visitation of the flock as well.

Miller's work includes a fascinating letter to "Christian Brethren." These are words to the members of churches to explain the work of the elders with a view to improving their understanding and to gain their cooperation. To the brethren on the matter of discipline, he wrote: "Your elders will some-times be called—God grant that it may seldom occur!—but they *will* sometimes be called to the painful exercise of disci-pline. Be not offended with them for the performance of this duty."[53] He also included information to members as to the elder's work of visitation: "When your elders visit your fami-lies for the purpose of becoming acquainted with them, and of aiding the pastor in ascertaining the spiritual state of the flock, remember that it is not officious intrusion. It is nothing more than their duty."[54] These quotations communicate both Miller's high view of the office of ruling elder and his view that ruling elders should be regularly involved in the oversight

52. Ibid., 17.
53. Ibid., 26.
54. Ibid., 27

of the flock. This reflected not merely Scottish influence but also strong biblical and theological convictions.

Summary

In summarizing this brief historical overview it can be concluded that the history of the church reveals a perpetual struggle over not only who leads the church but what leaders are supposed to do. The recognition of the authority of the ruling elder for the well-being of the flock of Christ was virtually lost from the third century to the sixteenth century. Even among the reformers there was reluctance to apply passages referring to "elders" and "overseers" (Acts 20; 1 Peter 5; 1 Tim. 3; Titus 1) to anyone other than the minister of the Word or teaching elder. The biblical basis for "ruling elders" or "governors" was limited to passages that spoke about the gifts of leadership or administration (Rom. 12:8; 1 Cor. 12:28). However, it is difficult to see how one can affirm the existence of the office of ruling elder and not apply the former texts to matters of calling, qualification, and function, given the complete biblical picture.

Though there continue to be differences in the understanding of the relationship between ruling and teaching elder, the Reformed churches, particularly in Calvin's Geneva and Presbyterian Scotland, laid the foundation for the importance of the office of the ruling elder alongside the teaching elder in caring for the flock. Together they are responsible to identify local membership and to provide ongoing care, nurture, and discipline of the flock.

Throughout its history, when a clear biblical understanding of the importance of the office of elder and its shepherding functions has been absent or impaired, God's flock has suffered. On the other hand, when leaders have sought to care for the flock, it has prospered.

For Further Reflection

1. Investigate the history of how the "offices" in your church came into existence.
2. If your church (denomination) has a book of church order, look up the descriptions of the offices in the church.
3. Does your context give appropriate weight to the office of ruling elder (or its equivalent)?

4

THE SHEPHERD'S BIBLICAL RIGHT TO LEAD: A FEW WORDS ABOUT AUTHORITY

"Obey your leaders and submit to them, for they keep watch over your souls as those who will give an account." (Heb. 13:17)

THE CONCEPT OF AUTHORITY is one that is increasingly alien to modern culture, and there may be any number of reasons that church leaders may shrink away from exercising authoritative shepherding leadership. It is important before moving on to what shepherds *do* that it is clearly understood that leaders have both the *right* and *responsibility* to exercise shepherding care. Before presenting the biblical perspective on authority, we will look at the challenges in the culture at large.

Following an introduction to the biblical concept of authority, we will examine two movements that have misunderstood the biblical view of authority.

"Who Says?" A Culture Adrift from its Moorings

The late George Carlin was once asked if he still supported the adage of the 1960s, "challenge authority." He answered in the negative and said that his new adage was "destroy authority." There would be many such as Carlin who would be quick to point out the abuses of authority throughout history, but G. K. Chesterton warned against throwing out the baby with the bathwater:

> Religious authority has often, doubtless, been oppressive or unreasonable; just as every legal system has been callous and full of cruel apathy. It is rational to attack the police; nay it is glorious. But the modern critics of religious authority are like men who should attack the police without ever having heard of burglars. For there is a great and possible peril to the human mind; a peril as practical as a burglary. Against it religious authority was reared, rightly or wrongly, as a barrier. And against it something certainly must be reared, if our race is to avoid ruin.[1]

It is unfortunate, but it appears that Chesterton's perspective is in the minority and that Carlin's view is no longer the fringe musing of an aging sixties pundit but increasingly represents the perspective of our society and, sadly, of the church.

1. G. K. Chesterton, *Orthodoxy* (Wheaton, IL: Harold Shaw Publishers, 1994), 31–32.

The deterioration of respect for authority in culture has its root in a failure to respect the sovereign lordship of the ultimate authority, the living God who is the Shepherd and authority of all of life. Though we pay great lip service to faith in God, the bottom line of our culture is not "the Lord is my Shepherd," but "I am my own shepherd." Respect for the authority of the Word of the Shepherd results in clear moral boundaries within which the sheep will be safe and secure. The sheep must look to the Shepherd to delineate the bounds of the "green pastures" and "still waters." It is to these standards that the shepherd-elder must be personally loyal and with which the elders must feed the sheep. Unfortunately, we live in a culture that has denied the authority of the Shepherd and the moral "fences" he has established. With the erosion of respect for the authority of the Shepherd, it is no surprise that respect for authority generally is diminished, whether in government, family, or the church. All of this together is symptomatic of nothing less than the deterioration of the foundation of lawful order in our culture.

> This is the cultural crisis—and therefore the political and legal crisis—of our society: the popularly accessible and vibrant belief systems and world views of our society are largely excluded from the public arena in which decisions are made about how the society should be ordered.[2]

Neuhaus continues in proposing that religion must fill the moral void left by the "naked public square." Unfortunately, respect for the authority of the church has diminished as well, particularly to the extent that the church has forsaken the authoritative

2. Richard John Neuhaus, *The Naked Public Square* (Grand Rapids: Eerdmans, 1984), 259.

standard of the Good Shepherd, accommodating its standards to the surrounding culture. As Chesterton further argues,

> . . . we can hear skepticism crashing through the old ring of authorities, and at the same moment we can see reason swaying upon her throne, In so far as religion is gone, reason is gone. For they are both of the same primary and authoritative kind . . . And in the act of destroying the idea of Divine authority we have largely destroyed the idea of that human authority by which we do a long division sum.[3]

With the loss of respect for authority, the basis upon which authoritative moral standards can be asserted in the public square or in the church has disappeared as well.

Doing What Is Right in Our Own Eyes: The Loss of Moral Values

In speaking of the fall of Communism in the Soviet Union, Os Guinness observed that it represented a dual victory for the American political order and economic order. But here's what he said about a "third" sphere:

> But the third great sphere . . . the moral and cultural sphere is in deep trouble. At the very moment of her historic political and economic vindication, a crisis of cultural authority is sapping the very vitality of the United States. Americans are no longer shaped by beliefs, ideals, and traditions as they once were. It is now questionable whether America's cultural order

3. Chesterton, *Orthodoxy*, 32.

is capable of nourishing the freedom, responsibility, and civility that Americans require to sustain democracy.[4]

The loss of respect for authority has led to the loss of authoritative standards. The loss of authoritative standards has left each person to be his own standard-maker. The sovereign authority of God has given way to the sovereign authority of the individual. Futurist Robert Naisbitt confirms the rise of individualism: "The great unifying theme at the conclusion of the 20th century is the triumph of the individual. Threatened by totalitarianism for much of this century, individuals are meeting the millennium more powerful than ever before."[5] In fact, in his concluding analysis of culture at the end of the twentieth century he says, "Recognition of the individual is the thread connecting every trend described in this book."[6] What are the implications of individualism upon morality? "The destruction of standards is inherent in radical individualism."[7]

This pessimistic conclusion is supported by the research of Patterson and Kim, who conducted a comprehensive survey of 2,000 Americans who responded to 1,800 questions. Here is one of their enlightening findings:

> Americans are making up their own rules, their own laws. In effect, we're making up our own moral codes. Only 13 percent of us believe in all of the Ten Commandments. Forty percent of us believe in five of the Ten Commandments. We choose

4. Os Guinness, *Dining With the Devil* (Grand Rapids: Baker, 1993), 16.

5. John Naisbitt and Patricia Aburdene, *Megatrends 2000* (New York: William Morrow, 1990), 298.

6. Ibid., 308.

7. Robert H. Bork, *Slouching Towards Gomorrah* (New York: Regan Books, 1996), 140.

which laws of God we believe in. There is absolutely no moral consensus in this country as there was in the 1950's, when all our institutions commanded more respect. Today, there is very little respect for the law—for any kind of law.[8]

The first chapter of Patterson and Kim's book is entitled "A New Moral Authority: You're It!" The question, "Who are our moral leaders now?" produced the following result: "Well, the overwhelming majority of people (93 percent) said that they—and nobody else—determine what is and what isn't moral in their lives. They base their decisions on their own experience, even on their daily whims."[9] This is nothing less than moral relativism. The picture is not unlike that portrayed in Judges 21:25, which states, "In those days there was no king in Israel: every man did that which was right in his own eyes." Without the authority of the king, the people became their own moral authority.

"We are living in what could be called a 'Me First' generation, whose primary interest seems to be to satisfy itself first, to do its own thing, to go its own way, to capture and hold on to absolute personal freedom, free from the restraints of law, discipline, self-denial, and self-control."[10] This perspective pervades our culture and has become a Madison Avenue selling point:

> The early pioneers were Nike's "Just Do It!" (in other words, don't think about it and don't let anything stand in the way to your doing it) and Burger King's "Sometimes, you gotta

8. James Patterson and Peter Kim, *The Day America Told the Truth* (New York: Prentiss Hall, 1991), 6.

9. Ibid., 27.

10. Paul Settle, "Of Church Censures 2: The Power of the Keys," *Equip for Ministry* 3 (1997): 16.

break the rules." And the imitator's have been numerous. Bacardi Black rum, which advertises itself as "the taste of the night," goes on to say, "Some people embrace the night because rules of the day do not apply"; Easy Spirit shoes even latched onto this theme promising a shoe that "conforms to your foot so you don't have to conform to anything"; Ralph Lauren's Safari celebrates "living without boundaries"; even stayed and reliable Merrill Lynch declares that "Your world should know no boundaries"; and Nieman Marcus encourages its customers to relax because, it says, there are "No rules here."[11]

Have any of these retailers considered the implications of their words? Imagine taking a trip to Nieman Marcus (which I'm sure you do regularly!), but this time you merely walk toward the door with your merchandise instead of to the checkout. Before you reach the door you are approached by a stern looking security guard who asks if you have paid for the items. You respond, "No." He informs you that you cannot leave the store without paying for them to which you say, "But I thought there were NO RULES HERE!" Do you think the security guard would say, "Oh, that's right. I forgot." I don't think so. Advertising phrases like these might sound good for marketing purposes as they capture the spirit of the day, but they really don't work out very well in day-to-day life.

Someone once said that "before you tear down a fence, you should find out why it was put there in the first place!" The authority of the Lord, the Shepherd, is no longer respected, and the natural consequence is the dismantling of the moral

11. David Wells, "Our Dying Culture," in *The Formal Papers of the Alliance of Confessing Evangelicals Summit* (April 17–20, 1996), 13.

principles and "fences" he has given us for our own good. The postmodern flight to relativism has ushered us into a *postmoral* age. As if that weren't bad enough, without the absolute standard of the Scriptures, the culture slowly deteriorates, becoming accustomed to each successive step downward. "With each new evidence of deterioration, we lament for a moment, and then become accustomed to it....As behavior worsens, the community adjusts its standards so that conduct once thought reprehensible is no longer deemed so."[12]

This downward trajectory of cultural standards places increasingly greater pressure on the church as it strives to maintain the clear moral imperatives of the Scriptures. Sadly, even those who are involved in the church are less and less influenced by their religious beliefs.

> When the pollsters go on to question how beliefs influence life, it becomes clear that for many people "belief" is little more than religious assent....They give conventional answers because they have never stopped to consider the implications of those stated beliefs for their manner of life. There is a disturbing gap between belief and personal commitment to those beliefs.[13]

Without a relentless commitment by the shepherd-elders to the authority of the Shepherd and his revealed will, the church cannot but parallel the moral decline of the culture, following eventually, but following nonetheless. Rather than being salt and light, influencing the culture with the truth, the church becomes the *influencee*, increasingly reflecting the godless values

12. Bork, *Slouching Towards Gomorrah*, 3.
13. Eddie Gibbs, *In Name Only: Tackling the Problem of Nominal Christianity* (Wheaton, IL: Victor Books, 1994), 30.

and priorities of its cultural context. Robert Bork's words are particularly lucid on this point:

> If a church changes doctrine and structure to follow its members' views, it is difficult to see the value of that church and its religion. Religions must claim to be true, and in their essentials, to uphold principles that are universal and eternal. No church that panders to the zeitgeist deserves respect, and very shortly it will not get respect, except from those who find it politically useful, and that is less respect than disguised contempt.[14]

However, those in positions of authority and responsibility in churches that "pander" are still accountable to God for the well-being of their flocks. Without clearly setting forth the boundaries and standards of the Chief Shepherd for the security of their sheep, the flocks are scattered:

> So they were scattered because there was no shepherd, and when they were scattered they became food for all the wild animals. My sheep wandered over all the mountains and on every high hill. They were scattered over the whole earth, and no one searched or looked for them. (Ezek. 34:5–6 NIV)

Without the will to assert the clear boundaries of God's standard, it is no surprise that the will is lost to seek for those who have strayed, since in so many cases church leaders do not even perceive that their people *have* strayed. What does it mean to stray if there are no fences? The implications for shepherds who are committed to seek stray sheep through church discipline are clear.

14. Bork, *Slouching Towards Gomorrah*, 293.

See No Evil, Hear No Evil: The Loss of the Will to Discipline

If there are no standards, what is there to enforce? If there are no standards, how can anything be "wrong"? Is it possible that this perspective has found its way into the church? The observations of Albert Mohler are particularly insightful on this point:

> . . . the modern secular worldview has wrought destruction within the Church as well. The modern attempt to dominate truth has given way within sectors of the Church to the post-modern rejection of truth itself. Indeed, in many denominations and churches, notions of orthodoxy and heresy have become "conceptual emptiness." The boundaries have vanished. The very possibility of heresy is dismissed in many circles within mainline Protestantism, and many evangelicals seem to have no better grasp of the moral imperative to honor the truth and to oppose error.[15]

If the boundaries have vanished between truth and falsehood in doctrine into a "conceptual emptiness," it follows that the boundaries of right and wrong *praxis* have given way to a "moral emptiness" as well.

In fact, the will to draw lines of right and wrong clearly and authoritatively has disappeared, and a newly found will has been found to stand *against* those who would *oppose* immorality: "In our day of diversity and tolerance, where God the Creator has been dethroned, denouncing error has become the ultimate unpardonable sin. Principial opposition to anything that others hold dear makes

15. Albert R. Mohler, "The Truth of God's Word," in *The Formal Papers of the Alliance of Confessing Evangelicals* (April 17–20, 1996), 3.

you a bigot and a hate monger."[16] The implications for discipline are clear. The leaders of churches that advocate certain aberrant lifestyles are in no position to discipline members who engage in such lifestyles. If the standards are self-generated, there is no ground upon which the church can stand to exercise discipline:

> This individualism, it is quite apparent in our time, attacks the authority of family, church, and private association. The family is said to be oppressive, the fount of our miseries. It is denied that the church may legitimately insist upon what it regards as moral behavior in its members.[17]

This result of these conditions is an increase of litigation by congregants against elders who may well be exercising their biblical responsibilities of church discipline.

> An increasing number of lawsuits against church officers signals a growing disrespect for the authority of Christ's officers. In many congregations it is acceptable for the pastor to denounce sin from the pulpit, but the officers are not to deal with specific sins according to biblical principles! This trend reflects a society which evidences increasing disrespect for authority and a rejection of absolutes, and which produces antipathy toward the erection and enforcement of absolute law.[18]

Unfortunately, the skepticism of lawful authority produces an authority without the *will* to discipline:

16. Peter Jones, "Apostasy in America: Dressing up Paganism in Christian Clothing in an Attempt to Take Over the Christian Faith," *Equip for Ministry* March-April 1997: 10.

17. Bork, *Slouching Towards Gomorrah*, 6.

18. Paul Settle, "Church Discipline: God's Way of Caring," *Equip for Ministry* July-August 2007: 16.

A fragmented society ... displays loss of nerve, which means that it cannot summon the will to suppress public obscenity, punish crime, reform welfare, attach stigma to the bearing of illegitimate children, resist the demands of self-proclaimed victim groups for preferential treatment, or maintain standards.[19]

A remarkably similar conclusion is reached by David Wells in speaking of the church's response to moral relativism:

It is, therefore, a matter of some poignancy to realize that in the very moment when our culture is plunging into unprecedented darkness, at the very moment in which it is most vulnerable, the evangelical Church has lost its nerve. At the very moment when boldness and courage are called for, what we see, all too often is timidity and cowardice.[20]

"Timidity" and "cowardice" are strong but accurate descriptions of shepherd-elders who fail in their commitment to the sheep and, ultimately, to the Chief Shepherd. This has led to a crisis of care in the church.

Today the church faces a moral crisis within her own ranks. Her failure to take a strong stand against evil (even in her own midst), and her tendency to be more concerned about what is expedient than what is right, has robbed the church of biblical integrity and power. It is true that, historically, the church has sometimes erred in this matter of discipline, but today the problem is one of outright neglect.[21]

19. Bork, *Slouching Towards Gomorrah*, 11.
20. Wells, "Our Dying Culture," 18.
21. Art Azurdia, "Recovering the Third Mark of the Church," *Reformation and Revival* Fall 2007: 61.

All of these developments have led to an increasing unwillingness of people to submit to authority or to make commitments to the institutions they represent, including the church.

The impact of cultural influences upon the work of the shepherd-elder is clear. Failing to acknowledge the sovereign authority of the Lord and his Word, the culture has wandered from any authority other than self. People are showing increasing reluctance to identify themselves with a particular flock, to make the commitment of church membership vows, and to submit to the authority of shepherd-elders inherent in those commitments. Even within the church, however, Christ's sheep are transgressing the bounds of safety and security established in his Word. Church leaders, on the other hand, are showing unwillingness not only to embrace the standards of the Chief Shepherd and his Word but reluctance to courageously seek those who have strayed for the glory of God and the health of his flock. The danger of the age in which we live is the collapse of commitment: to the Lord, to his standards, and to the authorities he has established.

For the church to function properly, we must understand and embrace the biblical nature and functioning of authority. This clearly has implications for those who are called to shepherd the church. Does anyone have a "right" to lead anyone else? What is the biblical basis for elders to shepherd the flock? Hopefully, the following "primer" on the nature and use of biblical authority will lay the foundation for leaders as they consider their responsibilities.

"Who Says?" An Introduction to the Nature and Use of Authority

What does the Bible have to say about authority? What does it have to say about the rights and responsibilities of leaders to exercise that authority? The New Testament speaks clearly of the existence and exercise of authority in the world. The Greek word "authority" (*exousia*) is rich in the biblical lexicography. At its most fundamental level *exousia* is the "right to do something or the right over something."[22] The biblical case must be made that elders, as God's shepherds, have *exousia*, "the right to act" on behalf of the Good Shepherd. There are five brief observations to be made concerning authority as it relates to the shepherd-elder.

1. All human authority is derived. "Then Jesus came to them and said, 'All authority in heaven and on earth has been given to me'" (Matt. 28:18 NIV). Ultimately, all authority is the Lord's. "All authority in the church belongs to Christ. From his place of authority at God's right hand, Christ gives the keys of his kingdom; he validates in heaven what is done in his name on earth."[23] In a later section, we will take a closer look at the concept of "the keys" as a human expression of God's authority. But the Bible is clear that only *God's* authority is underived. Any and every human authority is delegated from the Lord above. Paul writes, "Everyone must submit himself to the governing authorities, for there is no authority (*exousia*) except that which God has established. The authorities that exist have been established by God" (Rom. 13:1 NIV). Pilate claimed to have authority to crucify Jesus. Jesus reminded him, "You would have no power (*exousian*) over me if it were not given to you from above" (John 19:11).

The authority of the elder is from above as well. Paul reminded the Ephesian elders that the "Holy Spirit has made you overseers" (Acts 20:28). This note is echoed in Peter's words

---

22. Gerhard Kittel, *Theological Dictionary of the New Testament* (Grand Rapids: Eerdmans, 1964), 2:562.

23. Edmund P. Clowney, *The Church* (Downers Grove, IL: InterVarsity, 1995), 202.

as well. "Peter could not have warned the Asian elders against 'lording it over those allotted to your charge' (1 Peter 5:3) if they had no authority. As shepherds of the church, elders have been given the authority to lead and protect the local church."[24] All authority comes from the Lord and is exercised on his behalf. Ultimately, it is *his* authority.

2. The exercise of authority is designed to serve the well-being of those under its care. In referring to the authority of the civil authority, Paul writes, "he [the civil authority] is God's servant to do you good" (Rom. 13:4 NIV). Certainly, in the Lord's flock, leadership among God's people is always servant leadership. Peter writes that those who shepherd God's flock should do so "not because you must, but because you are willing, as God wants you to be; not greedy for money, *but eager to serve*" (1 Peter 5:2 NIV).

The Son of Man, the Chief Shepherd, came "not to be served but to serve, and to give his life as a ransom for many" (Matt. 20:28 ESV). The authority of the shepherd-elder must also be exercised for the well-being of the flock bought with Jesus' own blood (see Acts 20:28). In subsequent chapters, the specific responsibilities that shepherd-elders perform for the welfare of the flock will be outlined.

3. This authority is to be directed by God's Word. In the shepherd-elders' "right over" the sheep and "right to act" they are under the authority and direction of the Good Shepherd himself. Elders are responsible to look to him for wisdom and direction in caring for the flock. This wisdom and direction is to be found in God's Word through the illumination of the Holy Spirit. "Church

24. Alexander Strauch, *Biblical Eldership* (Littleton, CO: Lewis and Roth, 1995), 97.

authority, grounded in the Word of Christ, is also limited to it. Christian obedience to church rule is obedience in the Lord, for His Word governs the church, not the other way around."[25] Therefore, the exercise of authority in the church must always be grounded in the Scriptures and, conversely, loses its legitimacy when it calls those under its care to ignore, contradict, or contravene the truth found therein.

4. *All who hold derived authority are ultimately accountable to the One who gave that authority.* Inasmuch as the elder's authority or "right to act" comes from the Lord, it follows that they are answerable to him for the manner in which they act. It is an accountability to the Lord for their care for his flock. The writer to the Hebrews reminds his readers with the following imperative: "Obey your leaders and submit to their authority. They keep watch over you *as men who must give account* (emphasis added)" (13:17).

In commenting on this verse, Philip Edgecomb Hughes writes,

> They [leaders] are men who will have to give account to God, and this solemn consideration should affect not only the quality of their leadership but also the quality of the obedience with which the Christian community responds to that leadership.[26]

This concept is not new inasmuch as the "shepherds" of Israel were held accountable for their failure to care for God's flock.

25. Clowney, *The Church*, 203.
26. Philip E. Hughes, *Commentary on the Epistle to the Hebrews* (Grand Rapids: Eerdmans. 1977), 586.

"This is what the Sovereign LORD says: I am against the shepherds and will hold them accountable for my flock. I will remove them from tending the flock so that the shepherds can no longer feed themselves. I will rescue my flock from their mouths, and it will no longer be food for them" (Ezek. 34:10 NIV). As we saw earlier, rather than caring for the flock, these shepherds were taking care of themselves at the expense of the covenant people. Ideally, the final accounting to the Lord will result in blessing to the undershepherds of God so that "when the Chief Shepherd appears, you will receive the crown of glory that will never fade away" (1 Peter 5:4 NIV).

5. The flock is called to submit to the authority of the elders. Human authority is to be respected for the very reason that, ultimately, the authority is from the Lord.

> It is the Holy Spirit who has made them overseers, and they are delegated by the head of the church. It is the obligation of the people and the elders to recognize that the rule exercised by the latter is by delegation from Christ and to him they are responsible.[27]

This theme is made abundantly clear in the New Testament. The reason that citizens are to be submissive in paying taxes to the civil authorities is that "the authorities are God's servants, who give their full time to governing" (Rom. 13:6).

One of the characteristics of the Good Shepherd's sheep is that they hear his voice and follow him. In turn, they are to follow those shepherd-elders called by him and given authority over various folds in the world. Paul encourages

27. John Murray, *Collected Writings* (Carlisle, PA: Banner of Truth, 1976), 1:262.

the Thessalonian believers to "respect those who work hard among you, who are over you in the Lord and who admonish you" (1 Thess. 5:12 NIV).

> Them that "are over you in the Lord" is not an official description of a technical order of ministry, but it is difficult to see who could be meant other than office bearers in the church. The verb may be used of informal leadership, but it is also an official word, describing the function of those who are officers.[28]

Of great interest is the fact that the word translated in the New International Version for "respect" is the verb *eidenia*, a form of the verb *oida*, which means "to know." Here, it means, "respect, appreciate the worth of."[29] Paul adds, "hold them in highest regard in love because of their work" (1 Thess. 5:13 NIV).

The author of Hebrews encouraged his readers to "obey [their] leaders and submit to their authority" (Heb. 13:17). He says this is necessary not only for the sake of the leader, but for *their* sake as well. "Obey them so that their work will be a joy, not a burden, for that would be of no advantage to you."

> Christian leadership is intended for the *advantage* of all, not just for the advantage of those who hold positions of authority, and good and successful leadership is to a considerable degree dependent on the willing response of obedience and submission on the part of those who are under authority.[30]

28. Leon Morris, *The First and Second Epistle to the Thessalonians* (Grand Rapids: Eerdmans), 166.

29. James Frame, *A Critical and Exegetical Commentary on the Epistles of Saint Paul to the Thessalonians* (Edinburgh: T. and T. Clark, 1912), 192.

30. Hughes, *Hebrews*, 585.

Therefore, not only are the shepherds to know the sheep and take responsibility for them, but the sheep are to know, that is, to respect and appreciate, those who are over them in the Lord. This is the nature of the shepherd-sheep relationship with shepherds lovingly caring for the sheep and the sheep submitting to their loving leadership. This is the biblical framework within which leaders fulfill their responsibilities as shepherds. These principles should be taught within local congregations not only for the benefit of the "leadership" but in order that members will understand the importance of "followership," that is, that the proper exercise of authoritative leadership is for the benefit of the sheep and the glory of God.

Great vigilance must be maintained to assure that the biblical view is embraced and practiced. Unfortunately, there are always pressures to move to one extreme of the "authority continuum" ("lording it over" the sheep) or to the other (reluctance to embrace biblical authority structures). The closing section of this chapter will give an example of each "extreme."

The Pendulum Swings: Extremes on the "Authority Continuum"

The "Shepherding Movement" of a generation ago represents an example of the extreme of "lording it over" the sheep. The "emerging church" movement represents what I call a "flattening" of leadership structure and authority. These examples are instructive because they serve as reminders and warnings to us all that our sinful tendency is either to abuse authority or to neglect its proper use.

The "Shepherding" Movement

There may be some who in reading these pages about shepherding felt a knot in their stomachs and a skepticism born of difficulty in their own negative experiences at the hands of domineering church leaders. Jesus extended a clear warning about the inappropriate exercise of authority:

> You know that the rulers of the Gentiles lord it over them, and their great men exercise authority over them. It is not this way among you, but whoever wishes to become great among you shall be your servant. (Matt. 20:25–26)

In Peter's words to his fellow elders he reminded them that they were to shepherd the flock, "nor yet as lording it over those allotted to your charge, but proving to be examples to the flock" (1 Peter 5:3). Unfortunately, there have been too many examples where the biblical teaching about authority has been distorted into an inappropriate "lording it over" the people of God.

One such movement was the "shepherding movement" of the 1960s and 1970s. This movement was largely centered in charismatic churches and was motivated by the need for a greater focus on commitment, discipleship, and discipline among the surging numbers of the "Jesus Movement." Believers in each church were placed under the authority of house-group leaders who took responsibility to make sure that the members were fulfilling their commitments as believers. The house-group leaders were then accountable to the elders. So far, so good. The trouble began when practices such as "covering" were introduced. "'Covering' means that a church member must have any important decision, and sometimes less important ones, 'covered' or approved by their house-group leader, elder or pastor."[31] Again, this sounds innocent enough until the extent of the covering in some contexts is seen. "Examples of decisions for covering by an elder or more mature Christian are: moving home, employment, marriage, even an appointment with the doctor."[32]

Again, who wouldn't appreciate input on important decisions from an elder or a mature Christian? However, the difference is that such input was not merely recommended, but *required* by church leadership and was binding upon the church member. In some cases, the counsel of the elders was given the revelational weight of prophetic utterance. It is one thing for elders to provide counsel; it is another thing for them to dictate decisions for matters such as doctor appointments and the choice of marriage partners, claiming to be the revealed will of God. While the motives may have been good, the methods were not.

Other examples could be given of the "lording it over" extreme of the exercise of authority.[33] Unless properly understood in the context of the Scriptures, the authority of church leadership can deteriorate into cult-like control. Leaders must take their responsibilities seriously but must remember to exercise care, especially the care of church discipline, with constant reference to the directives and conditions set in the Word of God.

The Emerging Church Movement

If one end of the authority continuum demonstrates an overbearing "lording it over" the sheep, the other extreme is

31. Jerram Barrs, "Shepherding Movement," in *The New Dictionary of Theology* (Downers Grove, IL: InterVarsity Press, 1988), 639.

32. Ibid.

33. See, for example, Ronald Enroth, *Churches That Abuse* (Grand Rapids: Zondervan, 1992).

a reluctance to embrace and express authoritative leadership at all. One example of this reluctance can be found in various representatives of the emerging church movement.

Emerging movement leader Scot McKnight has proclaimed that "the emerging movement is an attempt to fashion a new ecclesiology [doctrine of the church]."[34] Upon what is this new ecclesiology to be based? At the heart of the emerging movement's view of leadership is that the "hierarchical" approach to leadership is severely flawed and is a vestige of the church's capitulation to modernism.

> What organizational structures did modernity hand to today's church leaders and members? During the twentieth century, the church, already hierarchical and rationalized, became even more so as it mimicked Henry Ford's hierarchical, assembly-line construction to maximize productivity, resulting in dehumanization and disempowerment. As the twentieth century progressed, characteristics of McDonaldized society reigned inside the newest forms of church as well.[35]

The driving concern of the emerging movement is the concept of authority or power of those in leadership. This criticism of "modern" leadership flows from the modern view that God is "a willful God who commands all reality through his awesome power."[36] The following conclusion emerges. "Modern churches resemble this modern God. Their leadership is based on power, control, and submission to authority. For the church to resemble

34. Scot McKnight, "Five Streams of the Emerging Church," *Christianity Today* February 2007: 37.

35. Eddie Gibbs and Ryan K. Bolger, *Emerging Churches: Creating Christian Community in Postmodern Cultures* (Grand Rapids: Baker, 2005), 20–21.

36. Ibid., 192.

the kingdom of God, current notions of church power must be drastically altered."[37] Ultimately, in view of this, "all previous power structures are made relative."[38] "Hierarchy" seems to be the bad word. Lest there be any doubt about this, "Emerging church leaders are opposed to any hierarchical understanding of leadership out of the conviction that it inevitably stifles people and creativity."[39] In asserting the need for the new model of network development Gibbs places the network over against the hierarchy:

> Rather than developing and replicating an organizational machine by way of an expanded bureaucratic hierarchy, network expansion is more akin to the growth of an organism. In this regard leaders have been likened to gardeners who plant, prune, fertilize, cultivate and harvest. The leader does not *control* but *cultivates*.[40] (emphasis original)

What does this look like?

> Emerging churches, in their attempts to resemble the kingdom, avoid all types of *control* in their leadership formation. Leadership has shifted to a more facilitative role as emerging churches have experimented with the idea of leaderless groups.[41] (emphasis added)

You can see that many in the emerging church movement have reacted to their view that any church structure is "modern"

37. Ibid.
38. Ibid.
39. Ibid., 194.
40. Eddie Gibbs, *Leadership Next* (Downers Grove, IL: InterVarsity Press, 2005), 63.
41. Ibid.

by not only "flattening" church structure but by a reluctance to move away from affirming those whom the Lord has called, gifted, and authorized to serve as leaders in his church in favor of "leaderless" groups.[42] It is fascinating to note that, in the discussion of the emerging movement, the expression "emerging *leaders*" is used without pause. How do these individuals become *recognized* as leaders? Who *authorized* them to speak for the movement? Is it because they are ones who have the most influence? As the saying goes, "if everyone is the leader, then no one is the leader." Unfortunately, in the effort to address "disempowerment," the very source of power and authority is at risk of being disempowered.

In all fairness, the concept of authority is not completely disenfranchised by everyone in the emerging church movement:

> Even in postmodernity, there can be no leadership without an appropriate exercise of authority. Such authority does not arise from a leader's position or title but originates in the trust built up on the basis of character, competence, respect, and consistency. Authority is based on the twin pillars of responsibility and influence, and leaders are not simply those who impose their own wills but are individuals from whom opinion is sought.[43]

While it cannot be disputed that such a description fits into the biblical picture of the *exercise* of leadership, it falls short in its description of how this leadership might *arise*, that is, the source of that authority. The authority of the leader does not "originate" or "arise" with the people but with the Lord.

42. See Rom. 12:8
43. Gibbs, *Leadership Next*, 66.

It is on that basis, and on that basis alone, that leaders can act with confidence.

The attempt of the emerging church movement to reverse the "disempowerment" of the people of God through deconstructing the modernistic hierarchy found in the church may just be throwing out the baby with the proverbial bathwater.

There is a great danger of doing disservice to the biblical view of authority and its ongoing exercise through the ages. The danger of abusing authority, on the one hand, and neglecting its appropriate exercise, on the other, are all too real. "Authority without compassion leads to harsh authoritarianism. Compassion without authority leads to social chaos."[44] Hopefully, this chapter will have introduced you not only to the cultural challenges facing those who would lead God's people but to a balanced biblical responsibility incumbent upon those who are called by him to shepherd the flock. Having laid this foundation we will now consider exactly what the shepherd is called to do.

For Further Reflection

1. What evidence do you see of the deterioration of respect for authority in the culture?
2. What evidence do you see for the deterioration of respect for authority in the church?
3. Why is a proper understanding of authority important in the context of shepherding the flock?

44. Timothy S. Laniak, *Shepherds After My Own Heart* (Downers Grove, IL: InterVarsity, 2006), 247.

4. Do you think that people of your church have a clear under-standing of the biblical principles outlined in the "Authority Primer?"
5. Do your officers have a proper view of their responsibilities as elders?
6. Can you think of other examples of the "extremes" on the authority continuum?

PART 2

SO WHAT'S A SHEPHERD TO DO? A COMPREHENSIVE MATRIX FOR MINISTRY

"He also chose David His servant and took Him from the sheepfolds; so he shepherded them according to the integrity of his heart and guided them with his skillful hands."
(Ps. 78:70, 72).

If you have been convinced that leaders in the church are to be shepherds, what are these shepherds to do? After all, "shepherd" is both a noun and a verb. It is not only something you *are* but something you *do*. Our study of the biblical foundations for the ministry of shepherding has already hinted at what these ongoing functions are, and in this section we will get into the details.

An Introduction to the Macro-Micro Distinction

In this section we will look at the fundamental responsibilities of shepherds. The Bible constantly compares God's people to real sheep. The categories identifying the needs of real sheep provide a wonderful analogy for what God's people need. Therefore, we will carry the biblical metaphor of shepherding over to our understanding of what shepherd-leaders do.

Different approaches have been taken to summarize the biblical functions that shepherd-leaders are called to fulfill. For example, Donald MacNair uses the acronym *GOES* (Guardian, Overseer, Example, and Shepherd).[1] Timothy Laniak uses the categories of provision, protection, and guidance.[2] For our purposes we will use the categories of *knowing*, *feeding*, *leading*, and *protecting*. These are not radically different approaches but different ways of capturing the same emphases. As we look at each of these fundamental functions, we will begin with a basic introduction to these sheep-intensive tasks, noting that these four functions address our most basic needs. This will be followed by a more detailed outline of those responsibilities under the categories of macro-shepherding and micro-shepherding. Let's take a few moments to look at this macro-micro distinction, which will help us get a clearer view of the responsibilities of shepherds.

1. See Donald MacNair, *The Practices of a Healthy Church* (Phillipsburg, NJ: P&R Publishing, 1999).

2. See Timothy S. Laniak, *While Shepherds Watch Their Flocks: Rediscovering Biblical Leadership* (Matthews, NC: Shepherd Leader Publications, 2007).

An Important Distinction: Macro-shepherding and Micro-shepherding

As I became increasingly convinced of the importance of the responsibility of elders to shepherd their flocks, I wrestled with the fact that there are important tasks that the elders are called upon to fulfill on a corporate, congregational level. On the other hand, the foundation of a shepherd's ministry must be in *personal* care and interaction with the sheep. The terminology of *macro-shepherding* and *micro-shepherding* is designed to help leaders understand and distinguish these comprehensive and complementary responsibilities.

The rationale for this distinction can be seen in Paul's moving farewell to the Ephesian elders. He reminded them that he "did not shrink from declaring to you anything that was profitable, and teaching you publicly and from house to house" (Acts 20:20). Paul's ministry was not merely in the *public* forum but in the *privacy* of people's homes. It was not merely corporate but personal. This balance must be maintained for an effective shepherding ministry, and it can be represented by this distinction between macro-shepherding and micro-shepherding.

Macro-shepherding refers to those important leadership functions that relate to the entire church. It has in view the elders' responsibility to provide "oversight" of the flock as a whole. Its concern is to address the corporate concerns of the congregation. There are important decision-making, vision-casting, and administrative functions that the elders must carry out for the health of the flock. As you will see, these macro-shepherding categories must be fulfilled for each of the basic shepherding functions. For example, under the shepherding function of "feeding" the flock, the macro-shepherding function is the elders' responsibility to oversee the comprehensive teaching and preaching ministries of the church.

Micro-shepherding, on the other hand, refers to the *personal* ministry of the elders among the sheep. It has in view the oversight of particular sheep for whom they have been given responsibility. Going back to the illustration of "feeding," micro-shepherding would be the elder's personal ministry of the Word to individuals and families. The micro focus is on developing relationships with the sheep and the exercise of shepherding functions on a personal level.

Unfortunately, many agree to serve as elders with the misconception that they are only being asked to serve in macro, corporate functions. Actually, many leadership training classes offered to prospective officers are clearly biased toward the macro functions. One result of this orientation is seeking and attracting elders who perceive of themselves as "decision makers" rather than "sheep lovers." This is not to suggest that these functions are mutually exclusive. However, there is grave danger to the health of the flock if the shepherds are not involved *personally* with the sheep. In fact, how can elders function properly on the macro level unless they are interacting with the sheep on the micro level? Rather, the seeds sown in personal ministry among the sheep bear fruit in enabling the elders to be more effective on the macro level. Below is a matrix designed to help you envision the various elements of the micro-macro distinction applied to the work of the shepherd. You can see the four primary shepherding responsibilities listed horizontally along the top with the macro and micro categories vertically on the left. The foundation for all of the functions in the ministry of the elders is the Word of God and prayer. As we proceed we will first identify the basic shepherding functions and then unpack them, progressively identifying the macro-micro distinctions in the matrix.

	Knowing	Feeding	Leading	Protecting
Macro Public/Corporate Ministry				
Micro Personal/Relational Ministry				
Prayer				
Ministry of the Word				

5

SHEPHERDS *KNOW* THE SHEEP

"I am the good shepherd. I know My own and My own know Me,
even as the Father knows Me and I know the Father."
(John 10:14–15)

THE PSALMIST'S PICTURE of the relationship between
the shepherd and his sheep teaches us how the Good Shepherd
meets four of our most fundamental human needs. When David
rejoices that "The Lord is my shepherd," he not only identifies that
we are relational beings but acknowledges the most important
relationship of all: the relationship with our God. It is for this
reason we begin with knowing and being known.

The relational dynamics in all of life must not be overlooked.
From the moment we are born, we desperately need the relational
bond with our parents. Throughout our lives we seek meaningful

relationships with family, friends, classmates, and co-workers. Eventually, most people long for marriage, the most intimate of human relationships. Ordinarily, loneliness and alienation from others are conditions to be avoided. Throughout our lives we grow in our awareness of the dynamics of "knowing" and "being known." From their earliest days our children want to know "who will be there that I know" when we inform them that they are going along with us to a particular gathering of people.

The most fundamental relationship of all and the foundation for all others is our relationship with the Lord. When God established his covenant with the children of Israel, he said, "I will take you for My people, and I will be your God" (Ex. 6:7). The same thought is seen in the Psalms: "Know that the LORD Himself is God; it is He who has made us, and not we ourselves; we are His people and the sheep of His pasture" (Ps. 100:3).

It is the Lord, by his grace, who has initiated this relationship. He calls us to himself, to know him and to walk with him. *The* model relationship is the eternal love within the Trinity: perfect unity, perfect communion, perfect love. In a mysterious condescension, the Son of God came into this world so that our relationship with the Lord could be restored. This loving initiative was essential because only he could address the primary barrier to our mutual fellowship: our sin. Jesus' death on the cross atoned for our sin and has restored fellowship with our God to all who believe in his work on their behalf. Jesus describes the mutual knowledge between shepherd and sheep that characterizes his relationship with his people. "I am the good shepherd. I know My own and My own know Me, even as the Father knows Me and I know the Father" (John 10:14–15). How remarkable that we have been called into this relationship with our shepherd!

It is our restored, loving relationship with the Lord that flows over into transforming our relationships with other people, particularly those who are also part of his flock. For the elder, as an undershepherd of the flock, this relational dynamic is crucial to effective care of the sheep. The general description of the responsibilities of shepherds must begin, therefore, with the dynamic of *knowing* the sheep. As we will see below, personal interaction with the sheep is fundamental to this element of shepherding. First, however, we will look at what it means to know the flock on the macro-congregational level.

Macro-knowing

What does it mean to know the sheep on a macro, congregational level? Before a shepherd can provide proper care he must know the *identification* of the sheep for whom he is responsible. Jesus not only identifies himself as the good shepherd, but also says, "I know My sheep and My sheep know Me" (John 10:14). Having reaffirmed this truth, that elders are Christ's shepherds and believers are Christ's sheep, some important questions come to mind. If elders are those who exercise authority over the sheep in the name of Christ, over which sheep do they exercise this authority? Does every elder have authority and responsibility for *all* the sheep? Conversely, to which shepherds (elders) do the sheep (Christians) have to submit? Does every sheep have to submit to every elder?

New Testament evidence clearly indicates that there are particular sheep for which particular shepherds are responsible. In most cases this relationship is expressed in the form of local churches. As we saw earlier, the elders exercise their God-given shepherding authority over particular believers in a particular place. This is the fundamental element of knowing the sheep in a macro sense. Knowing *who* is in your flock and knowing those for whom you are accountable is where shepherding begins.

The importance of this foundational mutual relationship between shepherd and sheep is established early in the apostolic ministry. Remember that Paul and Barnabas "appointed elders for them in each church and, with prayer and fasting, committed them to the Lord, in whom they had put their trust" (Acts 14:23 NIV). There were particular elders for particular churches. Paul "sent to Ephesus for the elders of the church" (Acts 20:17 NIV). He instructed Titus to "appoint elders in every town, as I directed you" (Titus 1:5 NIV). James urged those who were sick to "call the elders of the church to pray over him and anoint him with oil in the name of the Lord" (James 5:14 NIV). This text assumes a relationship between the sick person and a particular group of elders to whom they were to look for care. They were the elders who knew them and who were known by them. Peter used similar terminology when he urged elders to shepherd the flock "that is under your care" (1 Peter 5:2 NIV).

Macro-knowing requires that the elders are able to identify the sheep for whom they are accountable to the Lord. As shepherds, how do elders know the identity of these sheep? How do they identify the "members" of their flock? The shepherd's responsibility is to identify those who know the Good Shepherd, those who have heard his voice by responding in repentance and faith to the gospel of Jesus Christ. As John Piper says, "We do not *become* sheep by believing; rather we believe only because we *are* sheep."[1] This has implications for the elders' leadership in extending the gospel call to their respective communities.

1. John Piper, *Future Grace* (Sisters, OR: Multnomah, 1995), 215.

Believing that Jesus has died for his sheep and that they will respond in faith and repentance to the gospel call, elders will be diligent in mobilizing their congregations to extend that gospel call. Only his sheep respond to the call of the gospel. Jesus spoke quite pointedly to those who did not believe in him: "But you do not believe because you are not of My sheep. My sheep hear My voice, and I know them, and they follow Me" (John 10:26–27). Only by preaching the gospel to our communities will we know who, in his grace, are his sheep as they respond in faith. Jesus looked beyond his own day to the advance of his kingdom to every nation, tongue, and tribe. He told his disciples "I have other sheep, which are not of this fold; I must bring them also, and they will hear My voice; and they will become one flock with one shepherd" (John 10:16). In referring to these other folds Jesus was looking forward to the advance of his redeeming work beyond the Jewish people to the Gentile world. They will also come as they respond to the gospel of the risen Christ, regardless of race or language.

The elders are then responsible as they identify the parameters of their local church to discern as carefully as possible that those admitted to membership in the church of Jesus Christ are true believers, that they have truly "heard" the Good Shepherd's voice and have responded in faith. Putting it another way, the elders of a particular church are to do all that they can to assure the correlation between the visible church and the invisible church.

> The elders as a body (or session) are responsible for guarding the gates of the visible church. They exercise the keys of the kingdom of heaven for binding and loosing (Matthew 16:19; 18:18). It is their duty, ministering in Jesus name, to pronounce as repentant and justified sinners all who come

111

before them giving credible evidence of being born again to faith in Christ.[2]

While it is impossible to guarantee an exact correlation between the church visible and invisible, the elders are charged to make that determination as carefully as possible on the basis of the applicant's profession of faith.

At this juncture it is crucial to reiterate the source of the authority of the elders to make this determination. After all, who should have the "right" to determine who is, and who is not, a sheep? Who, if anyone, has the right to decide if someone can become a member of the church? This goes back to the "authority" issue discussed in an earlier chapter, but the concept of authority must now be applied to a very important aspect of church leadership. This is directly related to the "the keys of the kingdom" of which Jesus speaks in Matthew 16. These are the words that immediately follow Peter's identification of Jesus as "the Christ, the Son of the living God":

> Jesus replied, "Blessed are you, Simon son of Jonah, for this was not revealed to you by man, but by my Father in heaven. And I tell you that you are Peter, and on this rock I will build my church, and the gates of Hades will not overcome it. I will give you the keys of the kingdom of heaven; whatever you bind on earth will be bound in heaven, and whatever you loose on earth will be loosed in heaven. (Matt. 16:17–19 NIV)

A number of questions arise in light of these verses relating to the authority of shepherds in identifying Christ's sheep.

2. Lawrence Eyres, *The Elders of the Church* (Nutley, NJ: Presbyterian and Reformed, 1975), 15.

What are "the keys"? To whom are the keys given? Keys are symbols of authority, as F. F. Bruce observes: "The keys of a royal or noble establishment were entrusted to the chief steward or major domo; he carried them on his shoulder in earlier times, and there they served as a badge of the authority entrusted to him."[3] The expression is found in this sense in the book of Isaiah, speaking of the authority of Eliakim over the royal household in Jerusalem: "I will place on his [Eliakim's] shoulder the key to the house of David; what he opens no one can shut, and what he shuts no one can open" (Isa. 22:22 NIV).

In the New Covenant, Jesus is identified as the preeminent keeper of the keys, the one " . . . who is holy and true, who holds the key of David. What he opens no one can shut, and what he shuts no one can open" (Rev. 3:7). In both passages the keys have clear reference to opening and shutting. Keys have to do with access, with locking and unlocking. In granting the keys of the kingdom to the apostles, Jesus places in their care the guarding of the gate of the sheepfold. In Matthew 16, the reference is to the keys to the kingdom, and what is in view is access to the kingdom of heaven. The keys are to be used for "opening" and "shutting."

Ultimately, the exercise of the keys in opening the kingdom relates to the proclamation of the gospel of Jesus Christ.

> Thus we see, that the power of the keys, in these passages, is no other than the preaching of the Gospel, and that, considered with regard to men, it is not so much authoritative as ministerial; for, strictly speaking, Christ has not given this power to men, but to his word, of which he has appointed men to be ministers.[4]

3. F. F. Bruce, *The Hard Sayings of Jesus* (Downers Grove, IL: InterVarsity, 1983), 144.

4. John Calvin, *The Institutes of the Christian Religion*, ed. Ford Lewis Battles (Philadelphia: Westminster Press, 1960), 2:486.

In putting it this way, Calvin is asserting that their charge was not to "make sheep"—only the Chief Shepherd can do that—but to preach the gospel through which true sheep are identified, acknowledged, and admitted to the fold. The Westminster Confession of Faith puts it this way:

> To these [ecclesiastical] officers the keys of the kingdom are committed; by virtue whereof, they have power, respectively, to retain and remit sins; to shut that kingdom against the impenitent, both by the Word, and censures; and to open it unto penitent sinners, by the ministry of the Gospel; and by absolution from censures, as occasion shall require. (WCF 30:2)

This quote from the confession also addresses the authority of the holder of the keys to "shut" the kingdom. As indicated above, this occurs in two ways. First, failure to respond to the gospel results in the doors of the kingdom being "shut" to an individual. If someone does not "hear" the call of the shepherd, he is not Christ's sheep and does not belong in the sheepfold. Second, when the holders of the authority of the keys "put out" an impenitent sinner through censure. The exercise of the authority of the keys is spoken of in terms of binding and loosing (Matt. 16:19). This expression provides an important link in the use of the authority of the keys in Matthew 18, where the approach to one who has sinned is outlined. The initial step is to approach the offending party individually. If there is no resolution, then he is to take another with him. If that fails, the continuation of the process is outlined in this way:

> If he refuses to listen to them, tell it to the church; and if he refuses to listen even to the church, treat him as you would a pagan or a tax collector. I tell you the truth, whatever you bind

on earth will be bound in heaven, and whatever you loose on
earth will be loosed in heaven. (Matt. 18:17–18 NIV)

In this context, the issue is the authority to *exclude* someone
from the company of the faithful subsequent to their failure to
repent. Commenting on this text, Calvin sees the transfer of
spiritual authority over the covenant people from the Sanhedrin
to the church:

> Let it be observed, that the passage to which we have referred,
> relates not to the general authority of the doctrine to be
> preached . . . but that the power of the Sanhedrin is for the
> future transferred to the Church of Christ. Till that time the
> Jews had their own method of government, which, as far as
> regards the pure institution, Jesus Christ established in his
> Church, and that with a severe sanction.[5]

The authority of the keys in the New Covenant is exercised in its
simplest form to identify those who are truly Christ's sheep and
to exclude those who fail to profess faith or to remove those who,
having been once admitted, have proven not to be genuine.

It is not only important to understand what the keys are but
to identify who, if anyone, exercises such authority now. Roman
Catholicism traditionally holds that the authority of the keys
was given to Peter exclusively and then to those claiming suc-
cession through the papacy. However, biblical evidence supports
the exercise of this authority by the company of the apostles
and its perpetual exercise through the officers of the church.
"That the apostles as a group exercised this right [the keys] is
clear from the entire book of Acts. *All* did this on an equal basis

5. Ibid.

(4:33): there was no boss or superintendent."[6] If it is granted that the authority of the keys was entrusted to the apostles, can the jump be made to assert that the authority was then further delegated to subsequent generations of leaders in the church? The arguments to be marshaled for the continued existence and exercise of the authority of the keys flow not only from the Bible but from common sense.

It must be admitted that there is both continuity and discontinuity between apostles and elders and that both offices are referred to in 1 Peter 5:1. Peter reminds the elders of his apostolic qualification in describing himself as "a witness of the sufferings of Christ." Our previous look at this text, though, revealed that Peter referred to himself as a "fellow elder" (*sumpresbuteros*), emphasizing his identification with them as elders called to "shepherd the flock." He is recognizing not merely a continuity of function but also the authority to fulfill that function. "And, indeed, whoever will closely examine the words of Christ will easily perceive that they describe the stated and perpetual order, and not any temporary regulation of the Church."[7] While the foundational functions of the apostolate faded away with them, the Good Shepherd made provision for the ongoing care of his flock. John Murray summarizes the point quite clearly:

> Since the apostolate is not permanent, and since there is in the New Testament no other provision for the government of the local congregation, we must conclude that the council of elders is the only abiding institution for the government of the church of Christ according to the New Testament.[8]

6. William Hendriksen, *New Testament Commentary: Matthew* (Grand Rapids: Baker, 1973), 650.

7. Calvin, *Institutes*, 2:488.

8. Murray, *Collected Writings* (Carlisle, PA: Banner of Truth, 1976), 2:342–43.

The most basic responsibility of the shepherd is to know and identify his sheep. This is the exercise of the authority of the keys both in its "opening" and "shutting" functions as described above. "The keys were given to Peter as an apostle and elder, and therefore, to all the apostles, and then, when the apostles died, to all ordinary elders in the church."[9] The perpetual authority of the shepherd-elder is to watch and see that all who claim to be sheep make their entrance through Jesus Christ the gate. These then become those who are admitted to the privileges of membership, including the sacraments of the church.

> There are certain principles laid down in His Word which sufficiently indicate the terms of membership which Christ has enacted for His Church, and the character and qualifications of those entitled to be received into the Christian society, or to remain in as its members. And the first object which that particular branch of Church authority which respects discipline contemplates, is to execute the law of Christ in the admission to Church membership of those entitled to the privilege, and the exclusion of those who are not.[10]

Being baptized and receiving the Lord's Supper are the signs and seals of the grace of the New Covenant in Christ, and being admitted to them by the shepherd-elders is testimony that they are part of his flock, the covenant community.

This has decisive implications for the concept of formal church membership. On the basis of the profession of faith, the individual is recognized not merely as a sheep of Christ's

9. Paul Settle, "Of Church Censures: The Power of the Keys," *Equip for Ministry* May/June 1997: 16.

10. James Bannerman, *The Church of Christ* (1869; repr., Carlisle, PA: Banner of Truth, 1974), 2:291.

flock, but the shepherd-elder, exercising his God-given author-ity, "admits" him as a member of the local fellowship of believers under the government and care of the elders.

> It is not enough for us to say that we are merely a part of the universal or invisible church (all those who believe throughout the world, regardless of church affiliation). We must also com-mit ourselves to a local or visible group of God's people . . . the New Testament does not contain even a hint of someone who was truly saved but not a part of a local church.[11]

Edmund Clowney presents the following forceful argument for local church membership rolls:

> The lists of names in the book of Numbers give evidence of God's concern to define membership in his people; God's book of life is the archetype of the earthly register of his people (Ex. 32:32–33; Mal. 3:16). A prophetic psalm foresees the recording of Gentile names on the roles of Zion (Ps. 87:4–6). The names of Euodia, Syntyche, and Clement, recognized as members of Christ's body at Philippi, are in the book of life, according to Paul (Phil. 4:2–3). Matthias, chosen in the place of Judas, is numbered with the eleven apostles; those who were added to the church were numbered with the disciples, so that the total numbers could be set down (Acts 1:26; 2:41; 4:4).[12]

The confirmation of a new member's profession of faith by the elders is not merely a bookkeeping matter but encourages the

11. Wayne A. Mack and David Swavely, *Life in the Father's House* (Phillipsburg, NJ: P&R Publishing, 1996), 20.

12. Edmund P. Clowney, *The Church* (Downers Grove, IL: InterVarsity, 1995), 104.

member and affirms the validity of his profession by being admitted to the roll of the particular church.

It is through the identification of individual members with a particular congregation through profession of faith that the elders of that church *know* the sheep on the macro level for whom they will have to "give an account" (Heb. 13:17). "Church membership is an important matter, a way by which an individual believer can be put under the oversight of a particular body of elders as the New Testament requires. Thus the idea of a "membership roll" is a legitimate one."[13]

Along with the postmodern reluctance to commit to anything has come the emerging church movement's jettisoning of the idea of church membership. This is a capitulation to the growing reluctance of people to make a clear commitment by affirming "membership vows." Wade Clark Roof has made an extensive study of the largest segment of the current American population known as the "Baby Boomers:"

> Commitment is a problem in the sense that boomers tend to be fearful and suspicious generally—not just toward religion, but with regard to social attachments as a whole. But they are not anti-commitment ... They just appear to be that way as a result of the high levels of individualism and self-reliance within the middle-class boomer culture. Because they are more focused on self as the key social unit, rather than on family, church, or community, they are more introspective, figuring out what to give themselves to and where to place their energies.[14]

When questioning the validity of formal membership, this fundamental mutual relationship of the responsibility of the elder

13. John Frame, *Evangelical Reunion* (Grand Rapids: Baker, 1991), 100.
14. Wade Clark Roof, *A Generation of Seekers* (New York: Harper Collins, 1993), 184–85.

and the accountability of the sheep is not taken into account. The lack of a membership roll and the required oversight by the elders leads to administrative chaos, not to mention a scattered flock with no accountability or security. It is difficult to fathom how churches without membership rolls can ascertain the identity of the sheep for whom God has called them to care and for whom they will be accountable one day.

Therefore, the membership roll should be kept as accurate as possible, providing care to all, whether they are healthy, weak, stray, or lost. Sadly, these rolls are rarely viewed with this degree of seriousness. In many cases, membership rolls haven't been reviewed for years. Macro-knowing at its most fundamental level consists of clarifying the membership roll so that you will know the sheep for whom you will have to give an account to the Lord one day.

Macro-knowing the flock also includes more subjective matters such as understanding the unique characteristics of your congregation as a whole. If someone asked you to describe your church, what comes to mind? Is your church rural, suburban, or urban? Is it monocultural or multicultural? Is it a community church or a regional church? The answers to these and many more questions would help you articulate what you know and what you can express about your congregation as a whole.

Micro-knowing

If macro-knowing describes your knowledge of your flock as a whole, micro-knowing describes knowing the sheep personally. Not only does the biblical material speak of local elders and their responsibility to a particular flock, but we can infer from Peter's words a subsequent delegation of responsibility of specific sheep to specific elders within a local congregation as well. Peter admonishes the elders not to lord it over "those entrusted" to them (1 Peter 5:3). The word translated "entrusted" (*kleros*) sheds light on the scope of the work of the elder. The roots of this can be seen in its use in the Septuagint: "The use of *kleros*, found most frequently in Septuagint Numbers-Judges, suggests that the 'real estate' in the new community is the people themselves, clustered under caring guardians."[15] This served as the background for its use in the New Testament:

> In classical Greek *kleros* was an allotment of land assigned to a citizen by the civic authorities, the distribution frequently being made by lot. The term was therefore familiar to Gentile readers; while Jewish members of the Church would have found it still richer in meaning owing to its association with *kleronomia* [inheritance], a word already used in 1:4. The *kleroi* or spheres of pastoral care were the several parts of the spiritual *kleronomia* into which Christians had entered. The word "clergy" is derived from this.[16]

This interpretation is supported by others as well. Kistemaker confirms that *kleros* means "an allotment of members of the church."[17] Arndt-Gingrich notes that "the *kleroi* seem to denote the flock as a whole, i.e., the various parts of the congregation which have been assigned as 'portions' to the individual presbyters or shepherds."[18]

15. Timothy S. Laniak, *Shepherds After My Own Heart* (Downers Grove, IL: InterVarsity, 2006), 234.

16. Edward G. Selwyn, *The First Epistle of Peter* (Grand Rapids: Baker, 1981), 231.

17. Simon Kistemaker, *Peter and Jude* (Grand Rapids: Baker, 1987), 193.

18. William Arndt and F. Wilbur Ginrich, *A Greek-English Lexicon of the New Testament and Other Early Christian Literature* (Chicago: University of Chicago Press, 1952), 436.

While the practical implications of this for shepherding care will be explored in a subsequent chapter, it is important to note that particular elders were appointed to exercise their shepherding authority over particular believers in a particular location. This is where real shepherding happens. Every member should have a personal connection with at least one elder. Real sheep "know they belong to a shepherd. They are named, known, and counted every day."[19] The elders must not merely know the names of those members who are "his" sheep but must strive to know them *personally*. David Dickson captures the heart of knowing the sheep as he describes the relationship that should exist between the elder and his assigned flock:

> He must be acquainted with them all, old and young, their history, their occupations, their habits, their ways of thinking. They and their children should be their personal friends, so that they naturally turn to him as to one on whom they can depend as a kind and sympathizing friend and a faithful counselor.[20]

This relationship is the foundation upon which all other shepherding functions are built. In commenting upon Paul's ministry in Ephesus, Timothy Keller highlights the elements of personal ministry present in Paul's summary of his work in Acts 20:

a. Inspection (Acts 20:28): A pastor seeks to become intimately familiar with all the characteristics, circumstances

19. Timothy S. Laniak, *While Shepherds Watch Their Flocks*, 101.

20. David Dickson, *The Elder and His Work* (repr., Dallas: Presbyterian Heritage Publications, 1990), 15.

and needs of the people; the people should be conscious that their pastor knows them.

b. Visible Caring (Acts 20:31): A pastor shows that he loves and cares in his visitation. The pastor in his contacts seeks to be transparent enough so the people see how he feels (*"with tears"*). The pastor by his presence shows that he cares. By being available (*"night and day"*) the pastor expresses the love of the Good Shepherd.

c. Diagnosis (Acts 20:20a): Paul was careful to declare the profitable: he adapted his ministry to the "deficits" (needs) of the hearers. So pastors must move beyond inspection and caring and diagnosis. What are the specific spiritual conditions and spiritual needs? What are the person's deficits?[21]

An important intersection of macro-knowing and micro-knowing relates to the ministry of the gospel among your flock. Elders must know the sheep well enough personally in order to know whether they and their children have come to faith in Jesus. Have they "heard" and responded to the call of the Good Shepherd? Richard Baxter saw this as a primary responsibility in knowing the flock: "The work of conversion is the first and great thing we must drive at; after this we must labour with all our might. Alas! The misery of the unconverted is so great that it calleth loudest to us for compassion."[22] The development of a personal relationship with the sheep is most important at this point. Do you know for which sheep you

21. Timothy J. Keller, unpublished class notes. Used with permission.
22. Richard Baxter, *The Reformed Pastor* (1656; repr., Carlisle, PA: Banner of Truth, 1997), 94.

are accountable? Do you know them well enough to know if they, and their children, have come to faith in Christ?

Approaches to Micro-knowing

As we have seen, micro-knowing requires a personal relationship between the shepherd and the sheep. The sheep must know the shepherd and the shepherd must know the sheep. What can you "do" to foster this mutual knowledge among sheep and shepherd? The foundation of any shepherding plan must be the establishment of a relationship of trust and caring. A crucial measure to take in order to prevent member inactivity is to establish a system of regular, dedicated contact with members. These contacts represent the commitment of the elders to be proactive rather than reactive. This is a key consideration. If you ask members of most congregations, "When do you receive personal contact from your elders?" the two most common answers are "when there is a financial need or crisis" or "when I have done something wrong." Communication about these important matters must occur between elders and members from time to time. Wouldn't these contacts be more effective if such conversations were part of an ongoing, systematic series of communications between sheep and shepherd? When it is necessary to discuss these sensitive areas with the flock, isn't the likelihood of success higher where a relationship of mutual trust and respect has already been established? The commonplace, reactive approach is undoubtedly the reason that so many efforts to discipline the sheep fall short of success. When children only receive the attention of a parent when it is time for discipline, the results are often less than satisfying. A foundation of love, caring, and instruction is the appropriate context for effective parental discipline. The same is true in the church. A proactive, loving relationship with the sheep will lead to a greater likelihood (though certainly not a guarantee) of effectiveness in winning them back from error.

Another problem with a reactive approach is that it leads to the neglect of the healthy sheep. If you are only contacting members when they are negligent, when are the healthy sheep contacted for support and encouragement? After all, shouldn't those who are faithful in following Christ and supportive of the church receive the dedicated attention of the elders? Unfortunately, this is not the case in many churches.

The Advantages and Disadvantages of Home Visitation

How should the elders go about establishing regular contact with the flock? Earlier, it was seen that the answer of Richard Baxter was the systematic visitation of his members for the purpose of catechizing them. For many church leaders, where shepherding plans exist, visitation in the home is a common approach. The advantage of this strategy is that it is a dedicated face-to-face meeting with an individual or a family unit in their home. Much can be gained from this kind of interaction.

There are also disadvantages of this approach that can outweigh the advantages. Firstly, visitation in the home is usually infrequent. For example, most who adopt this approach commit to visit each family or individual member once per year. Is a once per year contact for an hour or two sufficient to establish the kind of ongoing communication that will foster mutual knowledge and trust? While it is possible that the discerning elder will be able to pick up signs of storm clouds, it is equally as likely, in the presence of lemon bars and coffee, that the members can keep up a "good impression" for an hour or two. The difficulties would then be left to grow unaddressed for another year, or until an emergency arises when the elders will have to respond reactively. The shortcomings of the annual visit were identified by Baxter himself:

> And, alas! How small a matter is it to speak to a man only once in a year, and that so cursorily as we might be forced to do, in comparison of what their necessities require. Yet we are in hope of some fruit of this much, but how much more might it be if we could but speak to them once a quarter, and do the work more fully and deliberately . . . . [23]

According to research done by the Christian Reformed Church, annual or even semiannual visitation falls far outside the optimal time within which sheep who begin to stray can be reclaimed:

> . . . the best time to reclaim disaffected members is within six to eight weeks. During this time the potential dropouts are in fact waiting for the church to pay attention to them so that they can talk about whatever is bothering them. After this initial two-month period it is much more difficult to re-involve such members. [24]

This confirms the necessity of a more frequent method of contact than the usual schedule of home visitation. If the visitation approach is adopted, it must be supplemented by another more frequent means of contacting the sheep. Another "frequency" problem is when a family is missed in any given year. Does this mean it will be two years between visits, or a year and one-half at best?

23. Ibid., 184.
24. Christian Reformed Church, *Building Bridges: The Art and Practice of Evangelistic Calling* (Grand Rapids: Church Development Resources, 1988), 66.

Secondly, the commitment to home visitation must take into consideration the likelihood of success. In my experience and interaction with scores of churches, the examples of such a visitation being completed are few and far between. In most cases, such an approach is developed with great enthusiasm, but as time passes, the motivation and schedules of those involved leads to a sense of defeat and guilt. Sadly, disappointed expectations can have a negative impact on the congregation. Having been told that they could expect to be visited, the call never came. Any failure to follow through on any plan can lead to guilty elders and frustrated sheep.

Thirdly, the contemporary cultural challenges to home visitation should be kept in mind. Richard Baxter carried out his visitation ministry in a largely agricultural setting. He could set out in the morning and expect to be able to meet with fourteen families in one day! "Two days every week my assistant and I myself took fourteen families between us for private catechizing and conference (he going through the parish, and the town coming to me)."[25] It is interesting to note that Baxter identified his work as "the town coming to me." His assistant was out and about in the countryside but families had the flexibility in those days to come to Baxter, and fourteen families two days per week! Such flexibility is incomprehensible to today's families and church leaders. Granted, there are contexts where daytime visitation is an option, but this is unrealistic in most congregations except, of course, for shut-ins and the elderly. During the day husbands *and* wives are involved in the workforce. Evening visitation isn't much more realistic with the busy schedules not only of member families, but elders' families, too.

25. *The Autobiography of Richard Baxter being the Reliquiae Baxterianae*, ed. J. M. Lloyd Thomas (London: J.M. Dent and Sons, 1925), 77–78.

A Humble Suggestion: Contact Members by Telephone

While grand plans of "every member visitation" should not be jettisoned without due consideration, it is crucial that an approach be embraced that is practical both for the elder and the member. One such approach is the use of the telephone. The advantage of using the telephone is that it allows for a frequency in communication not practicable in the home visitation format. It is actually very realistic, given a proper proportion of sheep to the shepherding team, to establish a goal of *monthly* contact for every family unit in the church. You can see that if for some reason the monthly contact is missed, hopefully the members will not go more than two months without a dedicated shepherding contact. Before shrugging off phone contact as the realm of telemarketers and political appeals, don't underestimate the impact of a personal call from someone who has concern for your well-being at the forefront.

Kindly consider this example. One evening I was enjoying a quiet evening at home and the phone rang. My wife picked it up and said that the call was for me. I picked it up and it was my dentist. I had been to his office for a routine check-up that day and he was calling to find out if I was doing alright after the appointment. I told him that I was fine. When I completed the call I asked my wife, "Guess who that was?" Obviously she didn't know. I told her, "It was Dr. Markowitz calling to see if I am doing alright. Can you believe that he would make a personal call to me just to see if I'm OK?" Needless to say I am always very impressed when he makes that phone call. It never ceases to amaze me that he would take the time *personally* to check up on me! Do not underestimate the impact of a personal phone call when people understand that you are calling to ascertain their personal well-being and to assess how you might be of assistance to them.

The difference between a telemarketer and a shepherding call is that the shepherd is calling for the benefit of the sheep. It is important that shepherding contacts are dedicated and purposeful and that the sheep know that this is the reason for the call. An opening greeting might be, "Good evening, Harry, this is Bill, and this is your monthly shepherding call." They immediately know the purpose of the call. You may even have prepared the member for the contact the previous Sunday by asking which evening would be best for you to call. If you get their voice mail, leave a friendly message indicating your purpose for calling and request that they call back. However, you should not wait for them to return the call—try to call back.

On one occasion, one of our families moved some distance away. (Remember, by the way, that your shepherding responsibility does not end for those who move away until their shepherding care has been transferred to another leadership team at another church.) I continued to contact them monthly but was always frustrated by getting voice mail. Every month I would leave a voice mail wondering if I would ever hear from them. After several months they were back in town and visited the church. I was glad to see them and they apologized that they kept missing my calls, but noted that just hearing my voice on their voice mail was an encouragement to them, and a reminder to affiliate with another church.

If you don't know how to begin these calls, simply express interest in the member's well-being and ask for prayer requests. The congregation should be prepared for these contacts, as you will see in a future chapter. Some might be reluctant or even suspicious at first, but persevere! You are carrying out your responsibility to serve your sheep. Be prepared to write down the prayer requests that they have. If you are contacting a family, be sure to inquire about each member of the family unit. You might take a moment at the end of the conversation to pray on the phone but, in any case, note the requests and pray for them throughout the month. You can see how this will be a natural conversation starter the next month as you ask for an update on the prayer request given the previous month. The sheep will be encouraged that not only did you remember their request but that you prayed for them.

Perhaps an issue will arise in your shepherding contact that you will need to respond to with further action. Remember, a faithful shepherd moves quickly to address the needs of the sheep. If they are bruised, wounded, or straying, you are now in a position to respond. Unfortunately, many church leaders don't even *know* that their sheep are hurting. Neither are they in a position to respond expeditiously before the situation deteriorates. Depending on the situation, you might need to contact the pastoral staff to assist in the response. In any case, be sure to check up more frequently and offer assistance. If deacons serve on your shepherding teams, they should be informed if their respective ministry is required as the result of a shepherding contact. The wisdom of including the complementary biblical office of deacon on shepherding teams is advocated in a subsequent chapter.

Your approach with each call will be influenced by your knowledge of the health of the sheep. For healthy sheep, use the shepherding call not only to obtain prayer requests but to encourage them and thank them for their faithful involvement in the ministry of the church. We are to "encourage one another day after day" (Heb. 3:13), and shepherds can set a wonderful example as they build up their sheep. Indeed, elders should be the CEOs (chief encouragement officers!) for their sheep. For members who are more on the periphery of church life, your call would provide an opportunity to help the member find a place of service in the church. You are merely helping them to keep the commitment made when they joined the church.

A challenge at first will be contacting stray sheep. Remember, you are responsible for *all* of the sheep on your membership roll. The initial call may be for the purpose of clarifying the member's status, but the elder should always ask for prayer requests. On one occasion I recall an initial conversation with a stray member who hadn't been in church for a couple of years. I explained what we were striving to do and asked for a prayer request. It was a somewhat awkward and brief conversation with no requests offered. The next month it was a very similar conversation. However, the third month, her son was going through some difficulties for which she requested prayer. Don't give up! As someone once said, "no one can stop you from loving them." This must certainly be the position of the caring shepherd. The love of the Good Shepherd must be extended through you even if it is unrequited.

An important advantage of this proactive approach to contacting the flock is that the communication lines are open to other matters that might need to be conveyed to the sheep. There might be a need to contact members about a particular congregational initiative or financial need. In this approach, however, it is the exception and not the rule. In the monthly calls, the lines of communication are also open for members to have their questions answered about ministries, programs, or concerns that they might have.

The primary advantage of the phone contact approach is that the contacts are sufficiently frequent to establish a vital communication link that will lead to increased mutual respect and trust between shepherds and sheep. Below is a typical report from a church whose elders engaged in a commitment to make phone contact with their members:

1. The elders are encouraged, having received many expressions of appreciation simply for their effort in making the call.
2. We have been able to clarify the status of several wandering or lost sheep. (One elder saw a lost member return to worship the very next Sunday after the contact was made. This was more than just a coincidence.)
3. The elders report feeling a greater sense of importance, responsibility, and dependence on the Lord, especially in the difficult issues they discover in people's lives.
4. Elders bring an increasing number of specific prayer requests to meetings.
5. The elders are able to make more informed decisions about policy, programs, and our future since they are more in touch with the real needs of our people.

The advantage of more frequent, regular contact is that it provides a natural vehicle of communication when matters of importance to the congregation need to be addressed. Of primary significance, however, is the elder's growth in his knowledge of his sheep and being poised to be in contact naturally when an issue might arise that needs more concentrated shepherding attention. This regular, active contact is designed to be *proactive* in its care for the flock. Please remember that these are to be *dedicated* shepherding contacts, not merely passing in the hallway on Sunday morning with a "how are things going?" You demonstrate the seriousness of your concern by the dedicated monthly shepherding call.

Other informal interactions may well be used to follow up on the monthly conversation.[26]

In summary, as you consider this crucial matter of micro-knowing the flock, be sure that your plan includes sufficiently frequent contact so that you can build trust with members. In most cases, home visitation is not of sufficient frequency to accomplish the goal of knowing your sheep. However, supplementing monthly phone contacts with a realistic plan of home visitation would be beneficial, if practical.

What about the Large Church?

Those who are involved in larger churches may have wondered all along how this applies to you. Granted, the large church presents a challenge at the very outset as you seek to clarify the church roll. Reviewing the status of hundreds or even thousands of members can be a very daunting task. However, does the number of members in your church change the fundamental biblical principles we have elaborated earlier concerning the responsibility of the shepherds to care for the sheep? Of course not! The challenge is in how to develop a plan to provide care for every member of your flock, regardless of how large the church. The bottom line is that most elders in large churches will need help. If your church has "inactive" officers, recruit them to become part of the membership contact ministry. In many churches there are nearly as many inactive as there are active officers.[27] This would be a natural place to start to enhance the numbers on your shepherding teams.

26. Other technologies such as e-mail can also be employed to follow up on the dedicated shepherding calls. However, much is gained by maintaining the "voice" contact via telephone.

27. See "Implications for the 'Class System' or 'Term' Eldership" in chapter 7.

One example worth considering for the larger church is the shepherding ministry of Tenth Presbyterian Church in Philadelphia. Church members are delegated among the elders on a geographical basis, though Tenth strives to take advantage of other fellowship and affinity connections where possible. The members within a certain geographical area become part of that "parish" together with the officers in that area. Tenth, with its 1,400 members, is a good case study of maintaining contact between a limited number of elders and a large membership. They realized that they were going to need help in order to meet the goal of contacting every member every month. The solution they have embraced involves mobilizing non-officers in the work of contacting the flock. These individuals are known as "Tenth Community Assistants" (TCAs). Rev. Marion Clark summarizes the work of the TCAs with these responsibilities:

1. Contact every member under his watch monthly
2. Report monthly and as needed to Parish Elder(s)
3. Help connect member as needed to the church body[28]

At the same time there is no doubt where the ultimate accountability rests in that the stated purpose of the TCAs is "to assist the elders in their responsibility to provide pastoral oversight of the church flock." This is just one example of the creativity that must be considered in meeting the needs of a larger congregation. The elders' fundamental commitment to shepherd the Tenth flock can be seen in these comments from Rev. Clark:

Everyone *must* be cared for. Everyone *must* be treated as valued members of Christ's body. And I, for one, am determined that

28. Marion Clark, *Tenth Community Assistants: It's About Relationships.* Internal document of Tenth Presbyterian Church.

will happen here at Tenth Presbyterian Church. I don't want a single member of Tenth Church thinking that they are not cared for. Not one. At least not because no one asks about them. By this time next year, everyone will be able to say, "I have an elder who knows me and cares about me." Everyone will be able to say, "I know who will help me when in need." Everyone will be able to say, "This is how I am involved in the church," or "I know how to get involved when I am ready."[29]

It is important to note that Tenth has moved through a few approaches to reach this goal. The point is that they have never given up and are determined to fulfill their God-given responsibilities as leaders.

Do you have this zeal for your church members? If so, you will find a way to establish this accountable, relational connection with every member of your church. Where there's a will, there's a way!

For Further Reflection

Work through the Shepherding Matrix together as officers and answer the following questions related to *knowing the flock*:

Are we stronger in macro-knowing or micro-knowing shepherding?

Macro-knowing

1. Do you have a clear understanding of the sheep for whom you will have to give an account, i.e., do we have an up-to-date and accurate membership roll?

29. Ibid.

2. If your church has no membership roll, how can you know for which sheep you are accountable to God? Consider a process of membership in your church that will reflect the mutual commitments of members and leaders.

Micro-knowing

3. Do your sheep "know" their shepherds? Are you approachable?
4. What steps have you taken to establish personal relationships with your sheep?

	Knowing	Feeding	Leading	Protecting
Macro Public/Corporate Ministry	• Accurate membership roles • Knowing the flock's corporate strengths, weaknesses, traits, and opportunities			
Micro Personal/Relational Ministry	• Knowing the sheep personally • Knowing which elders are caring for which sheep • Strategy for regular, personal contact			
Prayer				
Ministry of the Word				

6

SHEPHERDS *FEED* THE SHEEP

*"I will feed them in a good pasture, and their grazing ground
will be on the mountain heights of Israel. There they will lie
down on good grazing ground and feed in rich pasture on the
mountains of Israel. I will feed My flock and I will lead them
to rest," declares the Lord GOD."* (Ezek. 34:14–15)

"I SHALL NOT WANT" (Ps. 23:1b) is the exclamation of a
sheep contented in his divine Shepherd. This expression undoubtedly refers to the comprehensiveness of the care received by those
who belong to the Lord's flock. Subsequently, David enumerates the
various elements required to nourish sheep. "He maketh me to lie
down in green pastures: he leadeth me beside the still waters" (Ps.
23:2 KJV). One author who was experienced with sheep wrote
that "green pastures are essential to success with sheep."[1]

1. Phillip Keller, *A Shepherd Looks at Psalm 23* (Grand Rapids: Zondervan,
1970), 45.

Provision is the second fundamental human need that is met by our shepherd. So much of our lives revolves around making sure that we have "enough." Will we have enough to buy a house, to send our children to college, or to retire? From the moment we awaken in the morning we seek nourishment, and then at noon, and then again in the evening!

With what does the shepherd-elder feed the sheep? Jesus reminded us that "Man does not live on bread alone, but on every word that comes from the mouth of God" (Matt. 4:4 NIV). "As Jesus' undershepherds, they [elders] guide his sheep to the green pastures of His Word and feed them spiritual food."[2] The Word of God is that which satisfies the souls of the people of God. This is the key to true contentment. Jesus quoted these words in the context of his temptation in the wilderness. After forty days of fasting, Satan knew exactly where to attack the Savior. Even as the Lord had provided for the needs of his flock as they wandered in the wilderness, so Jesus knew that his sustenance would come from his Father, who meets man's most basic need.

Meeting the need for God's truth is a key to the health and growth of his people. The "flock of Christ cannot be fed except with pure doctrine which is alone our spiritual food."[3] This must be a key concern for the shepherd-elder. Returning to the reinstatement of Peter (John 21), Jesus uses the simple word for feed *(boskein)* in two of the three responses to his assertions of allegiance. Trench comments on the use of *boskein*:

> Whatever else of discipline and rule may be superadded thereto, still, the feeding of the flock, the finding for them of spiritual

2. Simon Kistemaker, *Peter and John* (Grand Rapids: Baker, 1987), 194.
3. John Calvin, *Commentaries*, trans. John Owen (Grand Rapids: Baker, 1984), 22:144.

food, is the first and last; nothing else will supply the room of this, nor may be allowed to put this out of that foremost place which by right it should occupy.[4]

Remember that the Lord in Ezekiel's day indicted Israel's elders for failing to fulfill their responsibility to feed the flock:

> Son of man, prophesy against the shepherds of Israel; prophesy and say to them: "This is what the Sovereign LORD says: Woe to the shepherds of Israel who only take care of themselves! Should not shepherds take care of the flock? You eat the curds, clothe yourselves with the wool and slaughter the choice animals, but you do not take care of the flock." (Ezek. 34:2–3 NIV)

A fundamental responsibility of any and every shepherd is to assure that the sheep are well nourished.

What can an elder do to insure that his flock is well fed? As we apply the macro-micro distinction to feeding the sheep, you will see the breadth of the shepherd's responsibility.

Macro-feeding

Macro-feeding is the leaders' responsibility to oversee the public ministry of the Word of God. This not only includes the preaching of the Word from the pulpit but the ministry of the Word in education classes as well as in small group ministry. They are responsible to be certain that what is being presented in the public ministry of the Word is the unsearchable riches

---

4. Richard C. Trench, *Synonyms of the New Testament* (London: Kegan, Paul, Trench, Trubner, and Company, 1894), 86.

of the inerrant, inspired Scriptures. The Word of God is the food that will nourish and encourage the sheep. The elders of the church must assure that the public "Word" ministry of the church provides a healthy, well-balanced spiritual diet for the flock. The wise pastor will depend on *sola scriptura* as the food that is fed to the flock. It is only through the Scriptures that the sheep will be adequately nourished. It is only through God's Word that the flock will be able to withstand the attacks of the enemy of their souls. As many shepherds have drifted away from the staple of God's Word, their flocks have been malnourished, becoming gaunt and weak in their faith.

The pastor should also be concerned to represent *scriptura tota* (the whole counsel of God) in his preaching ministry. The best way to provide this balanced diet is through the systematic expository preaching of the Scriptures. Verse-by-verse preaching from whole books of the Bible serves many purposes, including the following:

1. It identifies exactly what is the heart of the Christian message. "We are not expounding a passage from either secular literature or a political speech or even a religious book, let alone our own opinions. No, our text is invariably taken from God's Word."[5] People can hear about politics, the environment, or the economy anywhere, and by people who are likely to be better qualified in these categories. What the sheep need is the food that their Good Shepherd provides in the inspired revelation of his Word.

2. It requires that the shepherd concern himself with the intent of the Divine author for every text. The Lord gives us the Scriptures

5. John Stott, *Between Two Worlds: The Art of Preaching in the Twentieth Century* (Grand Rapids, Eerdmans, 1982), 126.

with his purpose in mind. The faithful expositor will seek this purpose rather than yield to his own whims and impose his own agenda in the ministry of the Word.

3. It respects the integrity of the textual units given through the inspiration of the Holy Spirit.

> I point to the fact that no one ever thinks of teaching the textbook of any other science in any other way. What would be thought of the master who professed to teach a system of geometry or mechanics by commenting in a brilliant way on one and another apothegm selected from the author.[6]

Every text is within a context designed by the divine author. An effective preacher takes into account the larger textual unit, the context in the book as a whole, and its place in the overall span of biblical revelation.

4. It keeps the pastor from riding his favorite hobby horses. We are all human and have our own interests and even our affinities when it comes to biblical texts and doctrinal truth. You may have heard of the preacher who, at the end of every sermon, regardless of the text would add, "and now a few words about baptism." Moving systematically through the Scriptures will help provide a balanced diet for the flock and will also help us to avoid our "pet peeves"!

5. It requires the pastor to preach the "difficult" or obscure texts and "challenging" truths of the Bible. While there are truths that

6. R. L. Dabney, *R. L. Dabney on Preaching* (Carlisle, PA: Banner of Truth, 1979), 79.

we enjoy preaching, there are also those which are more contro-versial and we (or our people) might like to avoid. For example, many are eager to preach on the Lord's order for the family in Ephesians five, but prefer to stay clear of Paul's direct preaching about predestination and God's sovereignty in the first chapter. Faithful expository preaching requires that these hard truths be wisely fed to the flock. Your congregation will appreciate the fact that you give them the milk and the meat.

6. *Expository preaching will encourage both pastor and congregation alike to become students of the Bible.* As the preacher works through particular books of the Bible, the congregation will learn what to look for in the biblical text and how to apply it to their lives. Dabney writes, "A prime object of pastoral teaching is to teach the people how to read the Bible for themselves . . . he should exhibit before them in actual use, the methods by which the legitimate meaning is to be evolved."[7] Ferguson adds, "it is chiefly by the exegetical method of preaching that the individual pastor is most likely to grow as a student of Scripture, a man of God, and a preacher."[8] Those who are committed to the work of the weekly exposition of the Scriptures know the personal blessing gained from meditating on God's Word in preparation for feeding the flock.

7. *Expository preaching gives us boldness in preaching, for we are not expounding our own fallible views but the Word of God.* It is only based on this understanding that we can confidently declare the truth, identify sin, and appeal to the sinner. The promise of God is linked to his Word and not to our own wisdom.

7. Ibid., 81.

8. Sinclair Ferguson, "Exegesis," in *The Preacher and Preaching*, ed. Samuel T. Logan Jr. (Phillipsburg, NJ: Presbyterian and Reformed, 1986), 195.

For as the heavens are higher than the earth,
so are My ways higher than your ways
and My thoughts than your thoughts.
For as the rain and the snow come down from heaven,
and do not return there without watering the earth
and making it bear and sprout,
and furnishing seed to the sower and bread to the eater;
So will My word be which goes forth from My mouth;
it will not return to Me empty,
without accomplishing what I desire,
and without succeeding in the matter for which I sent it.
(Isa. 55:9–11)

This promise is of great encouragement for shepherds as they strive to feed the flock what they need to hear even though sometimes it might be hard to swallow.

8. It gives confidence to the listener that what he is hearing is not the opinion of man but the Word of God. It will build a sense of momentum among the congregation. They will want to return next week to hear what comes next. W. A. Criswell built the First Baptist Church of Dallas beginning at Genesis 1 on Sunday morning, continuing on Sunday evening and kept on going Sunday mornings and evenings for years until he finished the whole Bible.

9. It is of great assistance in sermon planning. When you plan a series on a book of the Bible, you don't need to wring your hands wondering what you are going to preach about next Sunday. Very few of us can live as courageously as Spurgeon who sent people home early Saturday evening and then climbed into his study to prepare for Sunday morning.

145

10. It provides the context for a long tenure in a particular place. If you are serious about preaching the whole counsel of God, it will take you a long time to preach through the entire Bible!

Having enumerated these benefits of expository preaching as a means of macro-feeding the flock, the prudent pastor will consult with his elders for their insights on the overall preaching diet for the flock. What is *their* perception of what the sheep need? This can be a sensitive area, and preachers tend to be rather proprietary about their pulpits! However, if elders are truly shepherds and are in touch with the needs of the people, pastors should be eager to get the input of their elders, though the ultimate determination should be left to the preacher.

With respect to macro-feeding, the elders should also be concerned that the educational ministry of the church is well-designed and effective. So often there is little rationale to the content of Sunday school classes or its coordination with other ministries of the church. Wise elders will oversee this important ministry to assure that the sheep are receiving the food that they need. The same can be said for the small group ministry of the church. Leaders of these groups should be well trained and responsive to the direction of the elders in choosing materials.

Micro-feeding

The elders must be equipped for the *personal* ministry of the Word among the people of God as well. This can include personal opportunities for Word ministries from involvement in small groups to personal discipleship. The elder should ask the Lord for wisdom to be enabled to apply the Word to strengthen, calm, and heal his sheep. Paul writes that those who aspire to be overseers must be "apt to teach" (1 Tim. 3:2), and this embraces both public and personal ministries of the Word. Training should be provided for elders to address the basic biblical questions that the sheep might have. They should certainly be prepared to present the gospel to those who might not have understood or received it.

Approaches to Micro-feeding

If micro-feeding addresses the elder's responsibility to minister the word *personally* to the sheep, how might this task be addressed?

Richard Baxter's approach to this ministry centered around the use of the catechism as a means of ministering biblical truth to the members of his congregation. This would have provided a systematic approach to biblical truth that benefited the members as well as Baxter, for whom it provided a plan to follow. The catechism also provided him an opportunity to interact personally with his people about the most fundamental concerns of the Christian life:

> If we can but teach Christ to our people, we shall teach them all. Get them well to heaven, and they will have knowledge enough. The great and commonly acknowledged truths of religion are those that men must live upon, and which are the great instruments of destroying men's sins, and raising the heart to God.[9]

In other words, we should strive at least to enable our people to understand the fundamentals of the Christian faith. Each

9. Richard Baxter, *Reformed Pastor* (1656; repr., Carlisle, PA: Banner of Truth, 1997), 113.

leadership team must decide whether you intend to approach members with a systematic engagement with the Scriptures (i.e., a catechism or similar method), or rather respond to the respective questions and concerns the members might have. Baxter identified these basic categories of believers to whom you must be prepared to minister:

1. *The Young and Weak.* This includes those who, though "of long standing, are yet of small proficiency or strength."[10] Unfortunately, Baxter observes that "this is the most common condition among the godly." The loving shepherd needs to provide encouragement to these sheep to grow in their faith through use of the means that the Lord has provided.

2. *Those who labor under some particular corruption.* These are believers who have a chronic struggle with a particular sin in their lives. It might be pride, sensual desire, laziness, or any number of other besetting sins. The caring shepherd will have the kind of relationship with the sheep in which they are comfortable in sharing these struggles. He will also be prepared to offer prayer, Scriptural resources, personal support, and accountability as they engage in the struggle.

3. *Declining Christians.* These "are either fallen into some scandalous sin, or else abate their zeal and diligence, and show that they have lost their former love." These cases require our careful attention and may well require the shepherding ministry of church discipline. Christians in this condition must be addressed not only for their own sake but also for the honor of

10. Ibid., 97.

Christ. These are often the sheep that we would rather ignore and who out of a sense of guilt have absented themselves from the fellowship of believers. Nonetheless, the caring shepherd must be prepared to seek these strays and to assist them in repentance and restoration. This is not easy work and, in fact, can be heartbreaking. Baxter comments that "much skill is required for restoring such a soul."

4. The Strong. These are individuals who are walking with Christ and serving effectively among the flock. As we saw earlier, all too often, these strong sheep are ignored since in many churches, "the squeaky wheel gets the oil." The strong sheep need encouragement to press on in their growth in Christ as well. Take time to acknowledge the Lord's work in their lives and to express thanks for their faithful service.

A Simple Suggestion: Focus on Fathers

According to the Bible, each family has an undershepherd as well. This undershepherd is the head of the family who has been given the responsibility to shepherd their little "flocks" in the name of Christ. Imagine the benefit to our churches if dads were equipped to provide every aspect of shepherding care. Baxter was concerned for this as well. "We must have a special eye upon families, to see that they are well ordered, and the duties of each relation performed."[11] Working with fathers on these fundamentals is certainly a good place to begin.

> . . . ask the master of the family whether he prays with them, and reads the Scriptures, or what he doth? Labor to convince

11. Ibid., 100.

such as neglect this, of their sin; and if you have opportunity, pray with them before you go, and give them an example of what you would have them do. Perhaps, too, it might be well to get a promise from them, that they will make conscience of their duty for the future.[12]

What better way to multiply the personal ministry of the Word than by equipping dads to pray and read the Scriptures with their families. Note that Baxter suggests that we "give them an example." How many of our families would be well fed if we merely gave some simple suggestions to their shepherds?

Get masters of families to do their duty, and they will not only spare you a great deal of labour, but will much further the success of your labours. If a captain can get the officers under him to do their duty, he may rule the soldiers with much less trouble, than if all lay upon his own shoulders. You are not like to see any general reformation, till you procure family reformation.[13]

In doing this you are not only multiplying the ministry of the Word among your people but helping fathers fulfill their God-given responsibilities. Undoubtedly, many elders will have to repent of neglecting this duty themselves in order to proceed with a clear conscience. This is progress, too, and a great place to start!

In summary, each leadership team must decide its own approach to micro-feeding. Will it be proactive in terms of providing specific devotional guides or catechisms to individuals and families, or will it be a more reactive approach in ministering the

12. Ibid., 100–101.
13. Ibid., 102.

Word to the needs of the members as they arise? Either way, the ongoing personal interaction of elders with members provides a vital means of ministering the Word of God to the needs of the people for their growth and development in Christ.

If you have any doubt about the fruitfulness of investing time in personally ministering the Scriptures to your flock, consider the following question, "When have *you* experienced the most growth as a believer?" For many of us this brings back thoughts of those who invested their lives in us personally in discipleship relationships. They spent time helping us understand and apply the Scriptures to our lives. A related question is, "When have you had the greatest impact on *another person's* spiritual growth?" Again, this will probably remind you of a new believer you helped, or another individual with whom you met to direct them to biblical solutions to challenges that they faced. Some things never change. Investing time to assure that your sheep are well-nourished requires effort, but such effort will bear lasting fruit in the spiritual growth of your flock.

For Further Reflection

Work through the Shepherding Matrix together as officers and answer the following questions related to *feeding the flock* together as officers:

Are we stronger in macro-feeding or micro-feeding?

Macro-feeding

1. Are your sheep getting a well-balanced diet in the public ministry of the Word?

2. Have you sought to coordinate the content of Christian education and/or small groups to contribute to the balanced diet required by your flock?

Micro-feeding

3. How are you going to approach the ministry of the Word in your contacts with your sheep?
4. Will you take a proactive approach with a Bible study or catechism, or will you simply make yourself available to address questions as they come up in your shepherding contacts?
5. What are you doing to equip fathers in your congregation to feed their little "flocks" at home?

	Knowing	Feeding	Leading	Protecting
Macro Public/Corporate Ministry	• Accurate membership roles • Knowing the flock's corporate strengths, weaknesses, traits, and opportunities	• Pulpit ministry • Christian education • Sacraments		
Micro Personal/Relational Ministry	• Knowing the sheep personally • Knowing which elders are caring for which sheep • Strategy for regular, personal contact	• Discipleship • Mentoring • Small group		
Prayer				
Ministry of the Word				

7

SHEPHERDS *LEAD* THE SHEEP

"He led forth His own people like sheep and guided them in the wilderness like a flock." (Ps. 78:52)

LEADING THE FLOCK is a key responsibility of the shepherd. "He leads me beside quiet waters. He restores my soul; He guides me in the paths of righteousness for His name's sake" (Ps. 23:2b–3). Once again, the psalmist addresses another fundamental human need; the need for direction and purpose in life. People always want to know "what's next." Where should I go to college? Where should I live? What kind of career should I pursue?

Throughout redemptive history, the Lord has proven that he is faithful in leading his people. He led his people out of bondage in Egypt, through the wilderness with the pillar of cloud by day and the pillar of fire by night, and brought them to the

Promised Land. Jesus, the Good Shepherd, came into the world and proclaimed, "I am the way and the truth and the life. No one comes to the Father except through me" (John 14:6 NIV). Through faith, he is now our shepherd, and we are called to follow him. "My sheep hear My voice, and I know them, and they follow Me; and I give eternal life to them" (John 10:27–28). As believers, we find life and purpose in him, and he promises to lead us in his way.

Leading is probably what comes to mind when most elders think about their responsibilities. Characteristic of this leadership is that it is motivated by the well-being of the flock, not for the leaders' gain. Peter describes this leadership as "not lording it over those allotted to your charge, but proving to be examples to the flock" (1 Peter 1:3).

The story is told about a group of tourists in Israel who had been informed by their Israeli tour guide, after observing a flock and their shepherd, that shepherds always lead their flocks from the front. He told his attentive listeners that they never "drive" the sheep from behind. A short time later they drove past a flock along the road where the shepherd was walking *behind* them. The tourists quickly called this to their guide's attention and he stopped the bus to step out and have a word with the "shepherd." As he boarded the bus he had a sheepish grin on his face and announced to his eager listeners, "that wasn't the shepherd, that was the butcher!"

In leading the flock shepherds must be motivated by love for the Lord and for the well-being of the sheep. It must be evident to the congregation that the leadership of the elders is exercised for the good of the people and not for the benefit of the leaders. Even when leaders are developing plans on the macro level, this should take into account their interaction with the sheep on the micro level.

Macro-leading

This is undoubtedly what most elders perceive to be their primary responsibility. Making decisions for matters that concern the congregation as a whole truly is an important task for shepherds. This includes setting the vision, mission, purpose, and policies of the church. This could be intimidating except that the Lord has clearly outlined the broad purposes of the church in his Word. He has told us not only who we are but what we are to do. Most church mission statements express these fundamental biblical purposes in one way or another:

1. Worship: the church is called to be a people gathered to give praise to the Lord for who he is and for what he has done.
2. Education: leading the people to grow in their understanding and application of biblical truth.
3. Fellowship: leading the people to grow in the understanding and use of their gifts in order to minister lovingly to one another as the body of Christ.
4. Evangelism: leading the people and equipping them to share the gospel of Jesus Christ with their friends and neighbors as well as supporting the cause of the advancement of his kingdom in the world.

Edmund Clowney's summary is another helpful approach. "The church is called to serve God in three ways: to serve him directly in *worship*; to serve the saints in *nurture*; and to serve the world in *witness*."[1] Churches may use different terminology than what is used in these summaries, but these general categories are always

1. Edmund P. Clowney, *The Church* (Downers Grove, IL: InterVarsity, 1995), 117.

evident where there is a commitment to fulfill the biblical purposes of the church.

The challenge for each group of elders in macro-leading is to determine how each of these biblical purposes is to be accomplished at this particular time, in their particular community, and with their particular congregation. This is the challenge of contextualization. While there are many ministry models that have been "successful" in their particular settings, it is unwise to assume that lifting one model and dropping it into your particular community with your particular people will recreate the same result. Unfortunately, this is often a common approach in church life. Many of us remember the excitement surrounding the explosive growth of the Willow Creek Community Church in South Barrington, Illinois. Innumerable churches attended conferences to learn the Willow Creek "model" but were disappointed when they didn't experience similar growth in their communities. They failed to take into account their communities and the congregations with whom they were called to labor. Valuable insights can be gained from such models, but wise leaders will be careful to consider their own context.

Leaders should strive to attain "balance" among the biblical purposes of the church but should expect that one of them might be stronger. This merely reflects the diversity of gifts of the pastor and people or the needs of the community. For example, a church with a gifted preacher in a university setting will often have a particularly strong education-teaching ministry. On the other hand, the gifts of pastor and people might lead a particular congregation to be strongest in evangelism and missions. While each church will likely be strongest in one area, it is the responsibility of the leaders to strive to build each of these important biblical purposes of the church.

Since these are fundamental functions of the church, it is desirable that the *structure* of the church clearly support their development. This addresses the question of *how* the elders will assure the growing health of the biblical purposes of the church. Many churches have developed a committee structure that reflects the importance of these elements of ministry (worship committee, outreach committee, etc.). These groups are often led by elders so that they provide guidance and counsel as they provide macro-leadership for the church. In some larger churches, it is often these key ministries that require securing paid staff to provide direction and oversight (music staff, minister of education, minister of outreach, etc.). Such staff should still work in close consultation with the elders of the church as they carry out their work.

Another approach is advocated by Donald MacNair as he suggests the formation of "Ministry Centers."[2] In his approach, the elders oversee and provide accountability for these ministries but do not "chair" them or even necessarily attend the meetings. The rationale for this is to give non-elders legitimate opportunities to exercise their gifts while freeing up the elders to minister as shepherds. Whether elders lead committees or not, every effort should be made to deploy church members in using their gifts for the good of the body of Christ. After all, an important purpose of leadership is "the equipping of the saints for the work of service, to the building up of the body of Christ" (Eph. 5:12).

A helpful exercise for church leaders is to take time to evaluate which of these biblical purposes of the church is the strongest and which is the weakest. It is also beneficial to get congregational input on this question. Elders should not only strive to make the most of the strengths of the church but to be proactive in addressing perceived weaknesses. This can be a painful process but is as important for the overall health of the church as a thor-

---

2. See Donald MacNair, *The Practices of a Healthy Church* (Phillipsburg, NJ: P&R Publishing, 1999), 171–87.

ough physical exam is to the health of the human body. No one enjoys the process, but it often reveals weaknesses that must be addressed for the health and well-being of the patient.

Micro-leading

Peter told the elders that they should prove to be "examples to the flock" (1 Peter 1:3). This is the most important leadership function that an elder exhibits. Failure here sabotages the rest. This begins by being example of Christlike character so that you can confidently say with Paul, "follow me as I follow Christ" (see 1 Cor. 11:1). What are the qualifications to serve as an elder in the church? Paul makes it quite clear in 1 Timothy 3:2–7 that the focus should be on godly character:

> An overseer, then, must be above reproach, the husband of one wife, temperate, prudent, respectable, hospitable, able to teach, not addicted to wine or pugnacious, but gentle, peaceable, free from the love of money. He must be one who manages his own household well, keeping his children under control with all dignity (but if a man does not know how to manage his own household, how will he take care of the church of God?), and not a new convert, so that he will not become conceited and fall into the condemnation incurred by the devil. And he must have a good reputation with those outside the church, so that he will not fall into reproach and the snare of the devil.

How many of these qualifications relate to matters of competence in ministry? Only "able to teach" relates to ministry skill.[3] All of the

3. The same can be said of the other list of qualifications for elder in Titus 1.

other qualifications clearly reflect the importance of godly character. It can be said with confidence that grace-generated integrity is the leader's most important asset. This is undoubtedly the reason that in his address to the Ephesian elders, Paul said, "Be on guard *for yourselves* and for all the flock, among which the Holy Spirit has made you overseers" (Acts 20:28). Paul understood that it was essential for the elders to engage in self-protection and self-care of their godliness in order to be effective as protectors of the flock.

The sheep will indeed need guidance individually from their elders. To whom are they more likely to come? Will they be more likely to seek counsel from one who demonstrates the wisdom in life of godly character or one who does not? The answer is self-evident and gives all the more reason for elders to trust the Lord to develop godliness in their lives.

Micro-leading also requires that elders know their sheep personally inasmuch as they will seek counsel for the various situations that arise in their lives. Sheep need to know to whom they should go and must have confidence that the counsel they receive will be in accordance with the Word and tailored to them.

Elders should also lead by example in participation in worship and the ministries of the church. In many cases elders will provide leadership in these ministries among the people.

The Heart of Micro-leading

As we have already seen, when many elders think about leadership they focus on the macro responsibilities of making decisions, setting vision, and creating ministry plans. However, we must zoom in even more closely on the importance of the leader's godly example in micro-leading and leadership for the well-being of the flock.

This is the reason that Baxter, for example, in *The Reformed Pastor*, gives an extended exposition of the first part of Acts

20:28, "Be on guard for yourselves . . ." *after* which he expands on the second part of the verse, " . . . and for all the flock . . . ." It is important to pay attention to your own growth in godliness and character in order to be effective in your ministry as a shepherd. After all, if they don't see that you are following the Good Shepherd, why should they?

Below you will see a graphic that pictures the comprehensive scope of the elder's life and ministry.

SHEPHERDING: COMPREHENSIVE FRAMEWORK FOR LEADERSHIP FORMATION

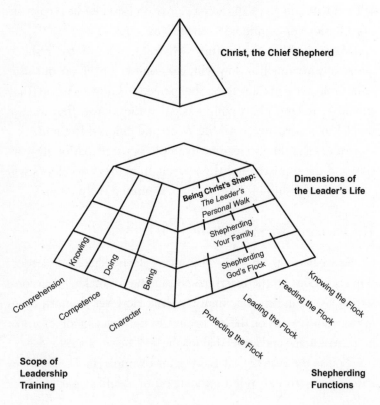

Christ, the Chief Shepherd

Dimensions of the Leader's Life

Being Christ's Sheep: The Leader's Personal Walk

Shepherding Your Family

Shepherding God's Flock

Knowing

Doing

Being

Comprehension

Competence

Character

Protecting the Flock

Leading the Flock

Feeding the Flock

Knowing the Flock

Scope of Leadership Training

Shepherding Functions

You can see that all is put in perspective under the lordship of Jesus Christ as the Chief Shepherd. You can also see the familiar shepherding functions on the right base of the pyramid (knowing, feeding, leading, protecting). Of importance to the discussion here are the Dimensions of the Leader's Life, which represent the horizontal layers of the pyramid. These capture the areas within which elders should lead by example.

Lead by Example in Your Relationship with Christ

Under the lordship of the Chief Shepherd, you must remember that you are a sheep, a follower of Jesus. This level addresses the matter of personal spiritual formation and growth. It must be clear to the flock that you *know* Christ personally and are growing in that knowledge. It would be wonderful if elders had the opportunity to give personal testimonies from time to time so that the sheep will understand how *you* came to know the Lord. You must also be committed to *feed* personally on the Word. Do you long for the pure milk of the Scriptures, or are you failing to be fed through your own personal neglect? Are you excited about the impact that the Scriptures are having in your own life, or are you in the "shredded wheat" (dry but nourishing) stage? Is it clear to the people that you look to the Lord to *lead* you in your daily life and in the larger decisions that you are called upon to make? You should also be an example of one who is diligent in heeding the warnings of the Scriptures, relying on the Lord to *protect* you from straying into sin or false doctrine. It should also be clear that you are submissive to the appropriate authorities in your life provided by the Lord for your protection.

Unfortunately, too many of us neglect these fundamentals of the Christian life, but it is the vitality of our relationship with the Chief Shepherd that is the source of our own growth and strength and that should be an example to the flock. If you are too busy to cultivate these fundamentals of the Christian life, you cannot be a good example to the flock. If you are too busy to cultivate the Christian life in this way, you are too busy!

Lead by Example as You Shepherd Your Family

The next level of the pyramid represents the leader's family life. The Scriptures are clear first of all that this is a basic qualification for leadership in the church. Paul wrote of those who would lead, "He must be one who manages his own household well, keeping his children under control with all dignity (but if a man does not know how to manage his own household, how will he take care of the church of God?)" (1 Tim. 3:4–5). Does this mean that a man must be a perfect father and husband? No. It does mean that if he is not handling the authority and responsibility in the home well, he is not qualified for undertaking the authority and responsibility of church leadership. Elders must lead by example in family living.

Putting it in the context of the shepherding pyramid, leaders must be good shepherds of their little flocks at home before they are qualified to serve as shepherds of God's flock, the church. He must do all that he can to see that his family has come to the knowledge of God through saving faith in Jesus Christ. When Paul writes to Titus that elders must have "children who believe" (Titus 1:6), he is not saying that an elder with a child who has not responded to the gospel is not qualified to be an elder. The child may yet come to Christ. It is also not saying that there can't be any "prodigals" among the children of elders. What it is saying is that these circumstances will be the exception and not the rule. It means that these circumstances may arise despite the fact that the elder and his wife have done their best to lead

164

the child by word and example to faith in Christ. On the other hand, there should be concern if *none* of the children of an elder have come to faith in Christ.

One way the elder can lead his family, and provide an example to others in the church, is to be sure that his family is *well fed* in the Word through family devotions. He should also value the opportunities that the church provides for the members of his family to grow. It must be clear that he is *leading* his family in the paths of righteousness, managing every aspect of his household according to biblical principles. He also takes seriously the responsibility to protect his family from harmful influences and the wiles of the devil. This protection should not only be proactive through instruction and warning but evident through godly discipline. Paul speaks about the elder "keeping his children under control" (1 Tim. 3:4) and who are "not accused of dissipation or rebellion" (Titus 1:6). The children of the elder should be respectful of his authority, and it should be clear that he has a good relationship with them.

The elder must also be an example of love for his wife. The bar has been set high, as husbands are called to love their wives "just as Christ also loved the church and gave Himself up for her" (Eph. 5:25). This is a high calling to selflessness and represents the essence of servant leadership. Your wife must know that you love and cherish her in this way. In a world in which marriage continues to be degraded, this will not only be a good example to the members of the church, but to the community at large.

In summary, you must be certain that your family holds the proper place of priority in your life. Remember that if your family life is not in order, a major qualification for leadership in the church has not been met. The temptation when an officer is to spend less time with your little flock, but you must be vigilant to guard this time so as not to compromise this fundamental responsibility, lest you disqualify yourself from shepherding the flock.

Lead by Example in the Ministry of the Church

The elder is to lead by example in his own walk with the Lord and as he shepherds his family. Moving down to the next level of the pyramid, the elder should also lead by example in the ministry of the church. He should be exemplary in the commitments that are expected of any member, supporting the worship and work of the church to the best of his ability. He should be using his gifts in ministry as his part of the body of Christ. Ask yourself, "If everyone was as involved in ministry as I am, how healthy would the church be?"

He should also be a faithful financial supporter of the church's ministry, though this is rarely information that is available to the congregation-at-large. Leaders should have confidence that, were this information made public, they would be exemplary and not embarrassed! Again, ask yourself, "If everyone gave financially as I do, would the church be solvent?" After all, how can you in good conscience urge others to be fruitful in these dimensions of life while not being a good example yourself?

In conclusion, the pyramid also depicts important elements of continuing development (bottom left), including comprehension, competence, and character. In too many cases, the emphasis falls on what elders *know*, instead of their abilities as shepherds or their godly character. It is essential that elders are vital examples of growth not only in the three dimensions of the leader's life but in the elements of continuing development, which together give a holistic picture of a faithful elder.

For Further Reflection

Work through the Shepherding Matrix together as officers and answer the following questions related to *leading the flock*: Are we stronger in macro-leading or micro-leading?

Macro-leading

1. Does your church have a mission statement that accurately reflects your understanding of the ministry of your church?
2. Do the ministries of your church represent a balance of the biblical purposes of the church? Which are the strongest? Which are weaker and in need of attention?

Micro-leading

3. Do you as leaders exhibit the character qualifications identified in 1 Timothy 3 and Titus 1, so that you can confidently say, "Follow my example as I follow Christ"?
4. Are your sheep comfortable coming to you for counsel and guidance when they are facing challenges and temptation?

	Knowing	Feeding	Leading	Protecting
Macro Public/Corporate Ministry	• Accurate membership roles • Knowing the flock's corporate strengths, weaknesses, traits, and opportunities	• Pulpit ministry • Christian education • Sacraments	• Vision casting • Mission and purpose • Ministry decisions • Committee leadership	
Micro Personal/Relational Ministry	• Knowing the sheep personally • Knowing which elders are caring for which sheep • Strategy for regular, personal contact	• Discipleship • Mentoring • Small group	• By example in personal godliness, family life, church commitments • Counseling	
	Prayer			
	Ministry of the Word			

8

SHEPHERDS *PROTECT* THE SHEEP

"Be on guard for yourselves and for all the flock, among which the Holy Spirit has made you overseers, to shepherd the church of God which He purchased with His own blood. I know that after my departure savage wolves will come in among you, not sparing the flock." (Acts 20:28–29)

THE FOURTH SHEPHERDING function reminds us of the fundamental human need for protection and security. Everywhere you go, from your car to a trip on an airliner, there are steps to be followed and safety measures to be enforced. Everything from our medications to our appliances has detailed instructions so that they can be used *safely*.

The Lord is the source of unshakeable security and protection for his flock. The psalmist has the assurance us that "even though I walk through the valley of the shadow of death, I fear no evil, for You are with me; Your rod and Your staff, they comfort me. You prepare a table before me in the presence of my enemies" (Ps. 23:4–5). He provides protection from the gravest danger of all, judgment for our sins. Jesus came to give his life for the sheep, delivering them from judgment and eternal death. He promises, "I give eternal life to them, and they will never perish; and no one will snatch them out of My hand. My Father, who has given them to Me, is greater than all; and no one is able to snatch them out of the Father's hand" (John 10:28–29).

Christ's undershepherds are called upon to protect his sheep. The challenge in protecting real sheep is that they are such a helpless lot. They only have teeth on one jaw, so the worst pain they can inflict on an adversary is a good pinch! This is why they need a strong protector. Shepherds need to be aware not only of the vulnerability and weaknesses of the individual sheep but also of the wolves that threaten their well-being.

Macro-protection

Sheep are very vulnerable creatures and can easily wander into danger. A few years ago the Associated Press reported a remarkable example of this from Aksam, Turkey. One sheep wandered over a cliff, then another, and then another. A total of 1,500 followed off the same cliff. The report continued:

In the end, 450 dead animals lay on top of one another in a billowy white pile, the Aksam newspaper said. Those who jumped

later were saved as the pile got higher and the fall more cush-
ioned. "There's nothing we can do. They're all wasted," [said]
Nevzet Bayhan, a member of one of 26 families whose sheep
were grazing together in the herd.[1]

A complaint against the shepherds of Israel (Ezekiel 34) and
the "hirelings" of John 10 was that pseudoshepherds ran away
when the flock was in danger. In contrast to this, David risked
his life for the protection of his flock by standing up against the
bear and the lion. The Good Shepherd gave up his life in order
to protect his flock from the ultimate eschatological danger: the
judgment of God.

Macro-protection is built on the foundation of public warnings from the Word of God. Paul warned the Ephesian elders
that "after I leave, savage wolves will come in among you and will
not spare the flock. Even from your own number men will arise
and distort the truth in order to draw away disciples after them"
(Acts 20:29–30 NIV). There will always be those who attempt
to influence the people of God for their own advantage. Often-
times their *modus operandi* is to "distort the truth" of Scripture.
The language that Paul uses is reminiscent of Jesus' warning to
his disciples: "Watch out for false prophets. They come to you in
sheep's clothing, but inwardly they are ferocious wolves" (Matt
7:15 NIV). The shepherd must be vigilant to see that not only
are the sheep well fed, but that they themselves do not become
food for "wolves." It is not surprising that Paul's challenge rises
to the words, "Therefore, be on the alert . . ." (Acts 20:31). F. F.
Bruce notes that "be on the alert" (*gregorueo*) is clearly a "pastoral

1. Associated Press, "450 Turkish Sheep Leap to Their Deaths," http://
foxnews.com/printer_friendly_story/0,3566,161949,00.html (accessed 31 Octo-
ber 2009).

word." To protect the flock requires great compassion for the sheep and courage to stand against harmful influences.[2]

Effectiveness in macro-protection includes an awareness of the particular cultural "wolves" that threaten the flock. Examples of those wolves might be materialism, sensuality, pluralism, relativism, and the panoply of sins flowing from them. In a culture saturated with these destructive values, the sheep not only need to be warned about the dangers but equipped to stand against them. Mrs. Herr of *Nix Besser* farm reported that she has to be particularly vigilant after a storm to remove branches and leaves that blow into her pasture from the neighbor's locust trees. Her sheep race to nibble on them because they taste so good. The problem is that they are toxic and can sicken and even kill the sheep. It is not uncommon that the things that are dangerous to Christ's flock not only look good but "taste" good, too.

Macro-protection would also include cases of church discipline that reach the stage where they are brought "to the church" (Matt. 18:17). This is an often-neglected responsibility of church leadership.

Micro-protection

The elders are called upon to "oversee" their sheep. The shepherd-elders are to keep watch in order that the sheep not stray from purity of doctrine or purity of life. Effectiveness in the shepherding function flows from the shepherd's knowledge of the sheep:

2. F. F. Bruce, *Commentary on the Book of Acts* (Grand Rapids: Eerdmans, 1970), 417n61.

We must labor to be acquainted, not only with the persons, but with the state of all our people . . . what are the sins of which they are most in danger, and what duties are they most apt to neglect, and what temptations they are most liable to; for if we know not their temperament or disease, we are not likely to prove successful physicians.[3]

It is essential to provide warning when necessary and to "go after" them when they stray. One of the most poignant pictures of the response of the loving shepherd to the wandering sheep is given in the gospel of Matthew:

What do you think? If a man owns a hundred sheep, and one of them wanders away, will he not leave the ninety-nine on the hills and go look for the one that wandered off? And if he finds it, I tell you the truth, he is happier about that one sheep than about the ninety-nine that did not wander off. (Matt. 18:12–13 NIV)

The discovery of stray sheep is not a matter for complacency but for decisive action. The likelihood of one of the sheep surviving on its own is of serious enough concern that the shepherd leaves the other sheep behind to find it.

Remember that central to the Lord's complaint against the shepherds of Israel was their failure to pursue the sheep who had wandered away.

You have not brought back the strays or searched for the lost. You have ruled them harshly and brutally. So they were scattered because there was no shepherd, and when they were

3. Richard Baxter, *Reformed Pastor* (1656; repr., Carlisle, PA: Banner of Truth, 1997), 91.

scattered they became food for all the wild animals. My sheep wandered over all the mountains and on every high hill. They were scattered over the whole earth, and no one searched or looked for them. (Ezek. 34:4–6)

The Urgency of Micro-protection in a Covenant Context

There is grave danger to the sheep that stray. In an earlier section, we saw that being identified and admitted into the fold as one of Christ's sheep by the elders of a church identifies the new member as part not only of his flock, but of the covenant community. This is wholly of God's grace and entitles those duly admitted to the benefits of membership including participation in the sacraments of the church. It also serves as a reminder of the member's covenant responsibilities. This is evident in the fact that members are admitted to the sealing ordinances of the New Covenant on the basis of their profession of faith *and* their commitment to follow the Lord. Therefore, the work of the elders in watching over the flock must be seen as far more serious than merely keeping the membership rolls accurate. The elders' work means keeping the sheep from straying from their covenant commitments and noticing when they do stray.

There are many examples throughout the Bible of those who were initially identified with the ranks of the covenant community but then proved themselves to be covenant breakers, those who did not bear fruit. From the very earliest days of biblical revelation, there are many notable examples of people who have been identified with God's gracious covenant relationship but have placed themselves in great peril by resisting the obligation of loyalty and obedience to their covenant Lord. As early as the first family we see the resistance of Cain to the gentle urging of the Lord to follow the way of blessing: "If you do well, will not your countenance be lifted up? And if you do not do well, sin is crouching at the door; and its desire is for you, but you must master it" (Gen. 4:7). However, he chose to go his own way, resulting in the pronouncement of a curse upon him. From within Adam's covenant family itself springs the humanistic line of the "Cainites." On the other hand, the godly seed is preserved through the giving of Seth, through whom comes righteous Noah. Though only Noah's faith is mentioned, his entire family is delivered through the watery judgment of the universal flood. However, shortly after the flood, with the emergence of the new humanity, a line of demarcation is drawn again within that covenant family. Ham, the father of the Canaanites, is cursed for dishonoring his father by observing his nakedness (and not covering it). From the very seed of Abraham comes Ishmael, one who received the sign of the covenant in circumcision but who strayed from the truth. "But what does the Scripture say? 'Get rid of the slave woman and her son, for the slave woman's son will never share in the inheritance with the free woman's son'" (Gal. 4:30 NIV). From the same womb, from the same parents, receiving the same signs of the same covenant were Jacob and Esau, of whom we read, "Jacob I loved, but Esau I hated" (Rom. 9:13).

This line of demarcation is drawn through the covenant community throughout redemptive history right through Jesus' day to our own. Amazingly, it was in the very presence of the leaders of the Old Covenant community that Jesus himself drew the line distinguishing between covenant keepers and covenant breakers.

> The Jews gathered around him, saying, "How long will you keep us in suspense? If you are the Christ, tell us plainly." Jesus answered, "I did tell you, but you do not believe. The miracles

I do in my Father's name speak for me, but you do not believe because you are not my sheep. My sheep listen to my voice; I know them, and they follow me. (John 10:24–27 NIV)

Those gathered around Jesus were "the Jews," children of the Old Covenant. They were standing in the very presence of the One of whom Moses and the prophets had spoken so clearly. But they did not believe or follow. Failing to believe in the fulfillment of law and the prophets, they became the object of condemnation. They failed to enter through the "gate" of the sheepfold, Jesus Christ himself. This line of demarcation cut through the covenant community not merely *to* Jesus' day but *through* Jesus' day to our own. Understanding the importance of covenant faithfulness does not compromise the truth of the security of those who are truly his sheep. It does, however, bring us face to face with the reality that not all in the fold are necessarily his sheep.

The seriousness of caring for the flock must impress the elder with a sense of urgency. "The New Testament warning that some in the church 'shall not inherit the kingdom of God' (Galatians 5:21; 1 Corinthians 6:9) is stunning. It is astonishing to me how many Christians are blasé about this matter."[4] What is even more astonishing is how many elders are blasé about this matter, as their sheep wander away from purity of life and doctrine. Elders must rather be diligent in attending to the health of the sheep and vigilant to continue to call them to faith in Christ and to covenant faithfulness. Think of the multitudes in our nation alone who have received the sign of the New Covenant in baptism but are now far from the Lord and his church. Where are the shepherds who should have been

4. John Piper, *Future Grace* (Sisters, OR: Multnomah, 1995), 249.

paying attention to the flock and especially those who strayed from the community of the faithful? These are sheep for whom shepherd-elders will have to give account to the Chief Shepherd one day.

Elders must know the sheep well enough to understand if they belong to the Lord and if they are walking with the Lord. One of the important biblical synonyms for elder is "overseer" (Greek, *episkopos*). This is a "visual" word that requires "watching" on the part of the elders, and it assumes that they are in a position to notice when sheep *begin* to stray. Ordinarily, there are certain commitments that members make when they join a church, such as attendance at worship and involvement in ministry. Most leaders identify the first evidence of straying as a change in attendance patterns. This is certainly something that shepherds can "watch" closely and respond to quickly when sheep begin to stray in this visible way.

Micro-protecting, therefore, must include the first steps of the process for winning back a stray sheep outlined by Jesus in Matthew's gospel:

> If your brother sins, go and show him his fault in private; if he listens to you, you have won your brother. But if he does not listen to you, take one or two more with you, so that by the mouth of two or three witnesses every fact may be confirmed. (Matt. 18:15–16)

These words outline how believers are to relate to one another, but they also provide direction to the elder as he goes about his work among the sheep. Shepherds must know their sheep well enough to notice when they begin to stray, that is, when they sin, and be ready lovingly to show them their error. The goal is always to "win" them back to the safety of the green pastures of the Lord's will. The words of John Murray should stir our hearts for the well-being of the sheep:

> How much of purity and peace would have been maintained in the church of Christ and will be maintained if elders are sensitive to the first steps of delinquency on the part of the people and bring the word of tender admonition and reproof to bear upon them before they reach the by-paths of open and censurable sin! A shepherd when he sees a sheep wandering does not wait until it reaches the well-nigh inaccessible precipices.[5]

An Important Element in Micro-protecting the Flock

On my visit to *Nix Besser* farm, I asked Mrs. Herr, "What is the shepherd's most important tool?" Of course, in my mind I had the romantic idea of the shepherd's staff that he would use to gently retrieve a wandering sheep. Or, perhaps, it was the rod that was useful in beating off predators. Over the years I have asked the same question to hundreds of students in my classes and scores of church officers who have gathered for training. They suggested such answers as "a dog" or "their voice" and, of course, the ones I suggested. They were all good possibilities, but Mrs. Herr's answer took me by surprise. She said clearly and without hesitation, "the fence." The fence keeps the sheep from wandering away. She added that if there were no fence, the sheep would merely wander away. Are you in a position to know when your sheep begin to wander away? Do you have any mechanism in place even to notice if they begin to stray? Is there

5. John Murray, *Collected Writings* (Carlisle, PA: Banner of Truth, 1976), 1:266.

any "fence" in your church? Let's look at a chronic problem and a simple suggestion.

Prone to Wander: Closing the Back Door

One of the great benefits of taking shepherding work seriously, particularly micro-protecting, is that it will help "close the back door." The "back door" is an expression used to describe the exit, often undetected, of members from our churches. Many churches are great at drawing a crowd and even receiving members, yet all too often the same church loses members as quickly as it is gains them. At the end of the year they are surprised when their attendance is basically the same as it was at the beginning of the year. Why is this the case? "I thought we received forty new members?" is the question often heard. The answer is simple: as new members are coming in the front door, others are moving out the back door, usually unnoticed, often becoming part of the "growth" of another church. This phenomenon happens not only from church to church but also on a much broader scale. For example, despite the publicity given to the exploding numbers of people flooding into mega-churches, growth of the church at large in the United States is essentially stagnant.

> Transfer growth, by definition, creates no numerical growth in the Kingdom of God. In fact the term is an oxymoron, and grossly misleading, for its net result is simply much ado about nothing. There are no new converts, no baptisms, no expansion of knowledge of God in the world, and no salvation fruit from this labor.[6]

6. William Chadwick, *Stealing Sheep: The Church's Hidden Problems with Transfer Growth* (Downers Grove, IL: InterVarsity Press, 2001), 30.

The truth of the matter is that much of the growth of mega-churches is drawn from smaller churches in the region. This is what I call the Wal-Mart effect. What happens when a Wal-Mart moves to town? Many small "mom and pop" businesses are forced to close because they can't compete with the prices, variety, and "one-stop shopping" of Wal-Mart. Likewise, small churches are depleted by large churches because the large churches provide "one-stop shopping" with ministries of every variety for everyone in the family. Sometimes the "prices" are cheaper, too. Not in the sense that a "tithe" is any less but that the anonymity of a larger church may not require the same level of commitment that smaller churches *must* have in order to function effectively. How many new members in your church are joining by profession of faith? How many are coming from other churches? These are important questions to consider.

The sheep shuffle from church to church, otherwise known as "church hopping." There is no doubt that there is a consumer mentality among many Christians whose primary question about a church is not, "Is this a good place for me to serve and where I can grow as a believer?" but rather, "Will this church meet my needs?" If you are on the receiving end of these new members you rejoice and consider it to be church growth and God's blessing. If you are on the losing end, you can easily become cynical and accuse other churches of "sheep stealing."

Many times when people are asked why they left a particular church they answer, "I wasn't being fed there." If the whole truth were told, most people don't leave because they are unhappy with the preaching but because they are not receiving the comprehensive relational shepherding care they need. Eventually, many of those who have been attracted by the ministries of a larger church will become disillusioned as the novelty of anonymity grows old and they realize that receiving shepherding care in the larger church is even less likely.

Well-shepherded sheep do not stray! If members know that their leaders care for them and are committed to know, feed, lead, and protect them, they will not be likely to look for "greener pastures" elsewhere. To be honest, one of the reasons that Wal-Mart continues to grow is that they not only provide good prices but customer service as well. There is someone there to greet you, guide you, and answer your questions.

An effective shepherding ministry will establish a connection between leaders and members in order to provide ongoing care for the sheep. This ongoing care and contact will provide a natural means of addressing concerns and conflicts that often lead to a "back door" exit. One of the primary reasons that sheep wander off is unresolved conflict with other sheep.

> Transfer growth creates a tempting and easy way out for those confronted by conflict. Rather than dealing with difficult issues and resolving the situation, they choose the nonconfrontational option of fleeing. When conflicts are addressed through escape, the church suffers many negative effects.[7]

When shepherding relationships are in place, elders will be in a position to serve as peacemakers and reconcilers among the sheep and hopefully will preclude them from moving toward the back door.

Established shepherding relationships also provide a natural communication link through which members can express concerns about other church matters. This enables direct, personal interaction with church leaders so that such matters can be

7. Ibid., 123.

clarified for the benefit of the sheep. In his book *Exit Interviews*, William Hendricks sought, through a series of interviews, to investigate the reasons for the massive movement of people from churches. One common reason was that no one ever knew about the concerns of the disgruntled members.

> I always asked my interviewees whether anyone had ever debriefed them on why they were leaving the church. Most of them said that no one had. In fact, a number of them told me that I was the *first person who had ever actively sought them out* to hear whatever they might have to say. I wonder: might things have come out differently if someone had simply listened to them as they were heading toward dropout?[8]

If you have a shepherding plan in place, your sheep will have someone to whom they can talk about their concerns before they even contemplate moving on. This is yet another benefit of having a proactive rather than merely a reactive shepherding plan.

A great advantage of staying in regular contact with the flock is that church leaders learn the vulnerabilities, challenges, and temptations with which members struggle. As the discerning shepherd gets to know his sheep, he should provide instruction, encouragement, and resources to help them face and triumph over these challenges.

A Simple Suggestion: Monitor Church Attendance

One of the first observable evidences of straying is a change in church attendance patterns. We have also seen that an effective response can only be made in a relatively brief window of

---

8. William Hendricks, *Exit Interviews: Revealing Stories of Why People Are Leaving the Church* (Chicago: Moody Press, 1993), 281.

time. Are you in a position to notice when there has been such a change in attendance patterns? This is important information that shepherds need in order to serve the flock well. The following scenario is all too typical:

> Craig and Amanda Donker's third and last child, Julie, graduated from high school in June and took a summer job to earn some college money. She moved in with some friends. Craig and Amanda celebrated this new stage in their life by taking most of the summer off for travel and vacation. During the entire summer it never seemed convenient to attend church. When September came around they drove Julie to college and resumed their normal working lives. Somehow the initiative to get up on Sunday morning was gone, and for several weeks they didn't even discuss it. When finally they did talk about it, Amanda said, "This may sound strange, but I haven't even missed church. We've been so busy and it seems nice to have Sunday just for ourselves." Craig replied that *he thought the pastor or someone else from the church should have called on them by now.* "After all the work we've done for the church over the past years, you'd think they would miss us. But nobody has even made a phone call." Before long, resentment over the church's negligence set in, and three months later the Donkers were firmly settled in their churchless life-style.[9]

You can imagine the progression of questions in church members' minds. After a few weeks absence they may ask, "I wonder if anyone has noticed our absence?" After a few more weeks the question becomes, "I wonder if anyone *cares*?" As we have seen earlier, as the absence moves to six to eight weeks

9. Christian Reformed Church, *Building Bridges: The Art and Practice of Evangelistic Calling* (Grand Rapids: Church Development Resources, 1988), 66.

without response, it becomes exponentially more difficult to win them back. Indeed, someone *should have* called the Donkers long before their resentment had an opportunity to develop.

If reduced attendance is a warning sign of straying, the shepherd-elder must have access to the attendance patterns of *his* sheep. If this is the case, then it is urgent that leaders develop a system for monitoring the attendance of members. Remember that one of the key synonyms for "elder" in the New Testament is the word "overseer." Many elders are not aware of the attendance patterns of members and, therefore, are not in a position to make a swift response to their absence. All too often, by the time a member's absence is noticed, it is well into the "difficult to re-involve" stage. Despite the fact that there is universal agreement about the importance of members' worship attendance, many churches fail to make an effort to keep track. Yet, this is one simple means of micro-protection, or in Mrs. Herr's words, of being the fence.

There are a number of different means in use to monitor church attendance. Some churches who keep attendance use "pew pads" which are located in each "pew" or row of the congregation. At a designated time, these pads are passed down the rows with hopes that *all* members and non-members alike will provide the information requested. This can be an effective tool for monitoring member attendance if members are faithful in filling out the form and if the information is provided to the appropriate elders for their response. Another tool used is a "tear-off" portion of the Sunday bulletin upon which information requested is similar to that requested on the pew pads. There are variations on the information requested, but the key purpose is to register visitors and to note attendance patterns of members. The disadvantage of both of these approaches includes the potentially monotonous routine of requiring attendees to tear and fill out the pad or bulletin form week after week. Inevitably, there are members who, for one reason or another, don't get the form filled out and passed in. There are also members, however few they may be, who object to this interruption of their worship experience. Another concern, in any attempt to monitor attendance, is that the information received is not processed properly or promptly. If this is the case, it is a waste of everyone's time and energy. If an "attendee registration" method is chosen, the obstacles can be overcome, particularly if the members know the rationale behind the request and there is an effective process in place to consolidate the information and distribute it to the elders in a timely fashion.

In another church, members have a mailbox in which their weekly bulletins are placed. Members are expected to clear out their mailboxes on Sunday. If the boxes are not empty at the end of the day, the members are presumed to have been absent, and the information is mailed to them. A shortcoming of this system is that a member just may have forgotten to pick up his information!

In other churches, attendance activity is tied to offering envelopes. One pastor reported that "if they [members] gave the same amount every month, they were deemed to have attended regularly." However, it is possible that someone could simply come once a month and present his tithe and never show up for the rest of the month. The shortcomings of this system are obvious.

A less intrusive yet reliable means of monitoring member attendance for most churches can be simply called the "eyeball" system. A list of all members can be placed on a bulletin board in a church office. For the benefit of the shepherd-elders, the list should be organized according to shepherding team assignments. Every week, the pastor and elders literally "take the roll" of those in attendance. At Crossroads Church, even with average Sunday morning attendance of more than 250 in two services, this exercise takes only a few minutes each week. It is very rare that someone is "missed" in this process. If there are multiple services, it is advantageous to have those who are involved in both services (usually pastors) double check the roll, which solves the problem of elders "missing" members by attending a different morning service.

Whatever the method used, it is important that the information acquired be put to good use and be readily available to the respective elders so that changes in attendance patterns be noted as quickly as possible. This information is immediately available to the elders (at our church, by looking at the board) and should also be reproduced and provided to them at the monthly officers' meetings.[10] In order for there to be effective shepherding, especially the prevention of inactivity, elders must be in a position to note changes in attendance patterns immediately. If you are skeptical about this approach, just ask yourself the question, "How else will you know?" Remember, the good shepherd in Matthew 18 was in a position to notice when only *one* of the one hundred in his flock was missing. A workable system of recording member attendance, therefore, will be a great help to elders as they keep watch over their sheep.

10. A sample of such a "Shepherd's View" sheet can be seen in appendix A. This form together with others mentioned in this book can be found online for download at www.theshepherdleader.com.

Conclusion

In this section you have been introduced not only to the basic functions of shepherds but to the important macro-micro distinction. The macro-shepherding category consists of the leadership responsibilities to the flock on a corporate, congregational level. The micro-shepherding category involves caring for the flock on a personal, relational level. Most leadership teams are more effective on the macro level than on the micro level. However, I am convinced that effectiveness in shepherding the flock (as you look at the comprehensive Shepherding Matrix) flows from the bottom to the top, from the micro to the macro level. After all, how can you know what the sheep need to balance their spiritual diets unless you are interacting with them on a personal level? How can you know the direction in which to lead the flock as a whole unless you are in touch with the gifts of the individual members? How can you effectively protect the church on a macro level if you do not know the challenges, struggles, and temptations that your sheep face?

Finally, you will notice that the foundation of the entire matrix is the ministry of the Word and prayer. The ministry of the shepherd to his flock must be grounded in the Scriptures both as the authority for ministry and the comprehensive source of truth to feed, lead, and protect the sheep. The elders, both individually and corporately,[11] must also be certain to commit the entire care of the flock to the Lord in prayer. We are completely dependent on the Lord for effectiveness as we work with his sheep for his glory.

11. Chapter 9 will include suggestions for the corporate prayer of elders for their sheep.

For Further Reflection

Work through the Shepherding Matrix together as officers and answer the following questions related to protecting the flock:

Are we stronger in macro-protecting or micro-protecting?

Macro-protection

1. Does your flock receive public warning against the particular cultural "wolves" they face along with tools to address them?
2. Do you take the responsibility of church discipline seriously as outlined in Matthew 18:15–20? Is your flock aware of the important principles for the peace and purity of the flock found in this passage?

Micro-protection

3. Do your sheep know you well enough to come to you when they have a problem?
4. Are you in a position to "notice" when sheep begin to stray from the worship and fellowship of the flock? What will you do to improve?

	Knowing	Feeding	Leading	Protecting
Macro Public/Corporate Ministry	• Accurate membership roles • Knowing the flock's corporate strengths, weaknesses, traits, and opportunities	• Pulpit ministry • Christian education • Sacraments	• Vision casting • Mission and purpose • Ministry decisions • Committee leadership	• Public instruction and warning from the Scriptures • Awareness of cultural "wolves" • "Tell it to the church" step of Matthew 18:17
Micro Personal/Relational Ministry	• Knowing the sheep personally • Knowing which elders are caring for which sheep • Strategy for regular, personal contact	• Discipleship • Mentoring • Small group	• By example in personal godliness, family life, church commitments • Counseling	• Private warning • Matthew 18:15–16 steps to restore wandering sheep
Prayer				
Ministry of the Word				

PART 3

PUTTING IT ALL TOGETHER

These final three chapters are designed to help you think about some important matters as you begin to put the concepts of this book into practice in your shepherding ministry. Chapter 9 focuses on seven essential elements of a shepherding ministry. Chapter 10 presents a simple summary outline of the steps to implement a shepherding ministry in your church based on the principles we have studied in the previous chapters. Chapter 11 discusses how to prepare the elders and congregation for the implementation of a shepherding ministry.

9

Seven Essential Elements of an Effective Shepherding Ministry

HAVING OUTLINED the importance of shepherding the flock and identified the biblical shepherding functions, it is crucial to develop a plan to carry out this important work. This chapter will focus on seven essential elements of an effective shepherding plan. Fail to include one of these elements and the plan will be deficient and likely to falter. If your church already has a plan in place, use these elements as an opportunity to improve what you are doing. Not only will each element be identified, but practical suggestions will be made for application. If your church does not have a plan, this section will provide what you need to get started.

193

1. An Effective Shepherding Ministry Must Be Biblical

Saying that it must be biblical should "go without saying," but it *must* be said because unless the shepherding ministry is founded on biblical convictions, it is unlikely to survive. There is no need to reiterate the details of the material presented earlier, but it is incumbent upon each group of officers to give serious consideration to this summary of the biblical foundations of shepherding. The scriptural references are not intended to be exhaustive.[1]

a. The Lord described himself as the shepherd of his people and his people as the flock under his care (Gen. 48:15; Ps. 80:1; 95:6–7).

b. The Lord's comprehensive care included knowing, feeding, leading, and protecting his sheep (Ps. 23).

c. Leaders of God's people such as Moses and David were described as shepherds of God's people (Ps. 77:20; 78:72).

d. Human shepherds were sometimes fallible and faithless (Ezek. 34:1–10; Jer. 23).

e. Jesus is the fulfillment of prophecy concerning the perfect messianic shepherd to come. In him his sheep find the ultimate provision, direction, and security (Ezek. 24:23–31; John 10:1–30).

f. Jesus provides for the ongoing care of his people through elders who are called to shepherd the flock (Acts 20:28; 1 Peter 5:1–2).

g. A plurality of elders is called to care for particular sheep in particular places (Acts 14:23; Titus 1:5; James 5:14).

1. See chapters 1 and 2 for a detailed development of these biblical principles.

h. Though the biblical terms for elder are synonymous, there is evidence that there are among the elders those who are particularly called and gifted to focus on the ministry of the Word of God. These elders share the responsibility for shepherding the flock (1 Tim. 5:17; Eph. 4:11).

i. Elders continue the shepherding functions of knowing, feeding, leading, and protecting the sheep. These functions are to be carried out corporately on the congregational level (macro) and personally among the people (micro) (Acts 20:20).

j. Shepherd-elders will be called to give an account for their care of the sheep one day and, therefore, the sheep are to respect their authority (1 Peter 5:4; Heb. 13:17).

ACTION PLAN

1. Have you studied the biblical material in chapters 1 and 2 and developed convictions about the importance of shepherding the flock?

2. Discuss the principles listed above.

2. An Effective Shepherding Ministry Must Be Systematic

To assert that a shepherding ministry must be systematic is merely to say that there must be a plan. If shepherding the flock is something elders are called to do, it is important to have a well-considered strategy to accomplish the task.

As we have already seen, Richard Baxter was a well-known advocate for shepherding his flock in Kidderminster, England, in the seventeenth century. He had a plan that, together with his assistant, enabled him not only to visit eight hundred families every year, but to catechize them! Remarkably, he accomplished this by setting aside two days per week in which he and his assistant each saw fifteen to sixteen families.

Do you have a plan for shepherding your flock? How effective is it? What do you need to do to improve it? Have you had one in the past? If it failed, why did it fail? If you have been discouraged in the past, don't give up on this important work.

Whatever plan you decide on should be realistic—it must be a plan that your elders are not only willing to do but able to do. For example, you might plan to visit every family in their homes twice a year. An important question is whether this is a realistic expectation of your elders *and* the families of your church, for that matter. You will also need to determine whether your plan is realistic in terms of your local cultural context. The essential elements that follow will help you to develop a detailed plan to shepherd your flock.

ACTION PLAN

1. Do you have a shepherding plan in place? If so, use these seven essentials to evaluate and improve your shepherding ministry.
2. If you don't have a plan in place, use these seven essentials to develop one.

3. An Effective Shepherding Ministry Must Be Comprehensive

To say that a plan must be comprehensive is merely to say that it must include *all* of the members of your church. Everyone on your membership roll should be included in the plan. Obviously, this may well require some attention to your membership roll. There may be people on the official roll who are long gone, or some who have more recently slipped away.

In any case, care must be taken in this exercise since each sheep on the roll was at one time acknowledged as a member of the flock on the basis of a profession of faith in the Good Shepherd. Remember, these are the sheep for whom you will have to "give an account" to the Lord one day. Attempts should be made to clarify the situation of each person on the roll and, where applicable, actions taken should follow denominational guidelines in light of biblical principles. Some who are unable to be identified or whose whereabouts are unknown may well be dropped from the roll. Others who are available to be contacted should be pursued with a view to winning them back to the church or transferring them to the care of the shepherds of another flock.

The "comprehensiveness" test is the element where most shepherding plans fail from the outset. Having had conversations with many church leaders over the years about shepherding plans, I first ask, "Does your church have a shepherding plan?" If the answer is yes, my follow-up question is, "How do you go about it?" The most common answer that I receive is, "We shepherd our people through our small group ministry." This sounds good initially inasmuch as it includes several important shepherding elements, such as the ministry of the Word and

197

an environment in which shepherds can get to know the sheep personally. However, there is an important follow-up question to the claim to shepherd through small groups: "How many of your church members are in small groups?" In exemplary cases, up to 60 percent of members might be involved in small groups. What is the next logical question? "How do you shepherd those members who are not in small groups?" This usually results in a blank stare or even a statement such as, "People who *want* to be shepherded come to small groups." Doesn't this put the burden in the wrong place? The responsibility to shepherd the flock is on the shepherds, not the sheep. Aren't the members who don't come to small groups often those who are in greatest need of the shepherding ministry of the elders? The point here is that most churches that claim to shepherd their people through small groups fail the comprehensiveness test.

On one occasion I asked this same question of the associate pastor of a very large church on the West Coast. His answer was, "Through adult fellowship groups." My natural follow-up question, then, was, "How many of your members are in small fellowship groups?" His answer: "I don't know." The comprehensiveness test breaks down again.

While small groups or larger fellowship groups might be an important *ingredient* in shepherding the flock, unless every member is involved, it fails the comprehensiveness test.

Application Plan

Before you can engage in an effective shepherding plan, you must know for which sheep you are accountable. At the most fundamental level and as discussed under macro-knowing, these are the sheep who are on the membership roll of your church. You must begin by gathering together as leaders to clarify the church roll. Sadly, there are very few churches in which the membership roll is without need to be updated. Set aside a Saturday morning or a special meeting of leaders to work through the membership list. As each name is read, clarify the circumstances of the individual. Unless the membership roll has been neglected for a very long time, someone among the leadership will have some recollection as to the situation of each individual on the roll. They may have been absent for a long time. They may be active members. They may be sporadic in their attendance. They may have moved away or moved on to another church. In each case, take note of the situation of each member.

A helpful exercise as you move through this process is to give a preliminary *diagnosis* of each sheep. Here is a suggestion:

1. Healthy sheep. This kind of sheep is one who is regularly in attendance in worship and is involved in ministering to others in some way. While the shepherd's ultimate goal is to ascertain the member's heart condition and encourage holistic spiritual vitality, worship attendance and ministry to others represent *observable* criteria and a good place to begin. One of the key concerns of Middle Eastern shepherds is to assure that the sheep are back in the fold every evening. "In traditional settings the animals are counted and inspected every night as they 'pass under the rod' of the shepherd."[2] In churches where prospective members are required to affirm membership commitments or "vows," a commitment to attend worship and be involved in ministry is usually included. They are expected to be present to worship their Lord. Many churches ask new members to affirm such a commitment by responding positively to a question such as

2. Timothy S. Laniak, *While Shepherds Watch Their Flocks: Rediscovering Biblical Leadership* (Matthews, NC: Shepherd Leader Publications, 2007), 157.

this: "Do you promise to support the worship and work of the church to the best of your ability?"[3] Such a question usually follows earlier questions in which the prospective member affirms his faith in Jesus Christ and his commitment to follow Christ. In other words, he has heard and responded to the call of the Good Shepherd, and intends to follow him. The commitments to support the worship and work are important visible pictures of a sheep following the shepherd with respect to the church, and these commitments have clear foundation in the Scriptures. Believers for millennia have gathered to worship their Lord, and this continues in the days of the New Covenant.

> And let us consider how we may spur one another on toward love and good deeds. Let us not give up meeting together, as some are in the habit of doing, but let us encourage one another—and all the more as you see the Day approaching. (Heb. 10:24–25 NIV)

This represents not merely a commitment to be in worship *somewhere*, but to be in attendance with the other members of that particular flock.

If you ask leaders, "What is the first evidence of member inactivity?" the most likely response is "they stop coming to church" or "they become sporadic in attendance." Gibbs identifies the highest degree of church commitment in his work on nominal Christians as that demonstrated by the "Active Regular Attender." This category, according to Gibbs, requires attendance at worship services "more than once a month."[4] However, this

---

3. This question is the fourth membership question affirmed by new members of a congregation in the Presbyterian Church in America.

4. Eddie Gibbs, *In Name Only: Tackling the Problem of Nominal Christianity* (Wheaton, IL: Victor Books, 1994), 32.

standard allows a member to be absent at least half the time and still be regarded as an "active" member. It seems that it would be more appropriate that the "healthiest" category of sheep include attendance at worship at least *more* than half the time. It is difficult to imagine an active, healthy sheep in attendance less than three Sundays per month, unless providentially hindered.

The biblical legitimacy of the commitment to minister is also easily demonstrated. Peter reminded believers that

> Each one should use whatever gift he has received to serve others, faithfully administering God's grace in its various forms. If anyone speaks, he should do it as one speaking the very words of God. If anyone serves, he should do it with the strength God provides, so that in all things God may be praised through Jesus Christ. (1 Peter 4:10–11 NIV)

Identifying with a particular local church is a commitment to minister together.

Paul's theology of the ministry of every believer affirms the importance of this commitment as well:

> Just as each of us has one body with many members, and these members do not all have the same function, so in Christ we who are many form one body, and each member belongs to all the others. We have different gifts, according to the grace given. (Rom. 12:4–6a NIV)

Paul is using "member" as an analogy to the "part" of a physical human body to focus on the importance of each person (see 1 Cor. 12:4–7). To affiliate with a particular local church is to make a commitment to minister within that context, to "belong" to that body. While all professing believers are members of the church universal, each one should also be a working part of the local expression of that body.

To "oversee" or observe the commitment to be in regular attendance and to be involved in ministry are legitimate starting points for diagnosing the flock and, in a sense, merely maintaining accountability for commitments the members have already made. Each leadership team will need to determine the standard for "regular" attendance and ministry to others. An active, healthy sheep should be in attendance every Sunday, unless providentially hindered. Ministry involvement should be broad enough to include informal personal ministry in which a member might be engaged and not merely limited to the "formal" ministry structure of the church. Each leadership team will have to make this assessment for their flocks. If a member can be identified as regular in attendance and involved in ministry, they can identified, for this initial diagnosis, as an active member or a healthy sheep.

While elders will need to probe more deeply into the spiritual condition of the sheep, these biblical categories for initial diagnosis are certainly better than some churches where an "active" member is identified as one who communes or gives financially merely once per quarter.

2. *Weak sheep*. This is the second category in the initial flock diagnosis. If a healthy sheep is one who is active in attendance and engaged in ministry, a *weak* sheep is one who is regular in attendance but who is not engaged in ministry to others. Sheep need exercise if they are to be healthy. There are many individuals for whom Sunday morning attendance is the extent of their involvement. They are designated as "weak" sheep because their concerns are limited to themselves. While they may feed regularly on the food served in the public preaching and teaching

ministry of the church, they receive no "exercise" in ministering to others. Not only are they missing the opportunity to grow through serving others, but the body of Christ is weakened by the absence of the ministry of this "member."

3. Stray Sheep. The stray sheep is one who is not only uninvolved in ministry to others but whose patterns of attendance are sporadic to the point where they may be seen only quarterly or less. These may fit into the category identified by many as "C-E" Christians, those who show up only on Christmas and Easter.

4. Lost Sheep. The lost sheep is one who has essentially forsaken the church altogether. This is an individual whose name on the roll is the only evidence of his connection with the church or the Lord.

5. Circumstantially Inactive Sheep. In addition to the previous four categories it is important to have a separate category in which to list members whose circumstances have led to their inability to be involved in the active life of the church. These would include those who are in nursing homes or shut-in, those away at college or in the military, in ministry or missions elsewhere, or who have moved away. In many churches "out of sight is out of mind," but these members also need the attention of the caring shepherd. Those who have moved away should be encouraged to become a part of another congregation in the vicinity of their new home. Shut-ins and those in nursing homes should be a regular part of the elder's contact ministry. Elders should contact those who are away at college, in the military, or in missions or other ministries in order to support them in prayer and become aware of their other needs.

As you undertake this examination of the membership roll and initial flock diagnosis, you may become discouraged. You may be dismayed not only by the number on the rolls who cannot be categorized as "healthy" sheep, but even more by the sheep about whom your leaders don't even have enough knowledge to make a diagnosis. Don't be discouraged! You have taken an important step in "knowing" your flock. The next step is even more important.

ACTION PLAN

1. Does your shepherding plan include *every* member of the church?
2. Do you have a clear understanding of the sheep for whom you are accountable? When is the last time that you clarified your membership roll? Set aside a meeting to work together through the membership roll.
3. Take time to complete the initial diagnosis of the sheep as suggested in this chapter.

4. An Effective Shepherding Plan Must Be Relational

As seen in the earlier biblical material, it is important for the sheep to know their shepherd and for the shepherd to know his sheep. The case has already been made that the plurality of elders in a particular church provides a ready-made structure for the establishment of relationships with the sheep. In order to

maximize the mutual knowledge of the shepherd-sheep relationship it is essential that the members of the church be delegated
among the elders of the church in order that each elder will
know which sheep he is responsible for and the sheep will know
the identity of their shepherd.

Delegate the flock

What rationale should be used for the delegation of the
sheep among the elders? There are a variety of methods
that have been used by various congregations. Immediately
following are four means used by various churches to "delegate" the care of the flock among the elders of the church.
These criteria will differ, of necessity, depending on the size
of the church.

1. By geographical area. Many churches use a geographical
approach to care for the flock. According to Pastor Marion
Clark of Tenth Presbyterian Church in Philadelphia, the care
of their 1,400 members has been divided among six geographical parishes. The parishes number in size from 80 members at the smallest to a high of 420 members in the largest
parish. These parishes are headed by "parish councils" which
consist of the officers within their respective geographical
parishes. These elders and deacons share responsibility for the
shepherding care of those within their geographical areas.

One disadvantage of this approach is that there will usually
be a heavier concentration of members in one geographical
area than others. A balancing consideration is that there will
probably be more elders in the area more densely populated
by members.

2. By fellowship groups. Other churches care for their flocks through fellowship groups or "mini-congregations." Paul Sailhammer, former senior associate pastor of the Evangelical Free Church of Fullerton, California, reported that the pastoral care of their 4,400 members is accomplished through adult fellowship groups. These groups number from 35 to 150 members, and church elders are involved in each of these groups, though they might not necessarily lead them.

3. By small groups. As we saw earlier, many churches identify small groups as their approach to shepherding the flock. Willow Creek Community Church in South Barrington, Illinois, strives to care for its membership through its network of small groups. This "meta-church" model for pastoral care requires individuals to identify with a small group *before* they can become members. At Willow Creek, a congregation of several thousand members, there are only six elders. This requires that most of the work of shepherding is delegated to others.

If the small group model of delegation is used, elders must be involved with the groups and actively engaged to assure that the overall plan includes every member in the church. As we saw earlier, the comprehensiveness test is probably the greatest challenge to the small group approach.

4. Elder "draft" selection. Elders in churches with memberships of up to 400 can easily "draft" members that they would like placed under their care. After the membership roll has been clarified, set aside another meeting for the purpose of holding a "draft" of the members by the elders. This approach is very effective inasmuch as it takes advantage of the natural connections elders already have with church members. Simply work systematically through the

206

list of members and allow the elders to choose whom they would like under their care.[5] For example, "Harry Abernathy" might be in elder Smith's small group. This would be a natural draft for elder Smith. Elder involvement in small groups can be a great asset to a shepherding ministry as they provide personal interaction between shepherds and the sheep. It is not even necessary that these groups be elder led but merely that the elder is involved. Another connection might be if a member has worked closely in a ministry led by another elder. This would be a natural choice for that elder. There are other natural connections of affinity and friendship that would be the basis of an elder's draft choice. You will find that this process moves quickly and may even lead to some brotherly "bickering" and rival claims over some members. Could you make a concession based on a future draft pick? You will find that this process is quite exciting and enjoyable as you get down to the important work of making sure that every member of your flock is accounted for.[6]

It is important for you to remember to include the "stray" and "lost" sheep in your draft. They will need to be contacted to clarify their relationship to Christ and to the church. The importance of the earlier diagnosis becomes clear now as you must make sure that a single elder doesn't become overburdened with an unusually high number of "difficult" cases and "lost" sheep. Again, when drafting these members, take into account the relationships that particular elders currently have or may have had in the past. Success in contacting these sheep will definitely be aided by some relational connection with an elder. Those members for whom there is no relational connection should be equally divided among the

5. It is best to work through the membership roll by family units.
6. See appendix A for a sample form to use to delegate the flock. Also available online at www.theshepherdleader.com.

eldership. Remember, you are accountable for *every* sheep entrusted to you by Christ. Don't forget to repeat this draft process when new members are added. Be sure to pay attention that the sheep are as evenly distributed among the elders as possible.

Whatever the method employed, the shepherd-elders must know *exactly* the sheep for which they are responsible, even if that care has been delegated to another level of leadership (small group leaders, minichurch leaders, etc.). It must also be comprehensive in scope—it must include *all* the sheep.

What is a realistic number of members for an elder to oversee? The ideal number would be between ten and fifteen family units. This would include a family as one unit and a single person as one unit in coming to the total. This number is not set in stone but is merely a practical suggestion based on years of experience. When the numbers climb higher than this, it can become difficult and cumbersome. Hopefully, by the time your little flocks reach this number the Lord will have raised up additional elders to assist in the shepherding ministry.

Include Deacons

What part, if any, should deacons have in the shepherding ministry of the church? It is clear from 1 Timothy 3 that the office of deacon is perpetual for the benefit of the flock. Paul's letter to Timothy includes qualifications for both the offices of overseer (elder) and deacon.

It is not the purpose of this study to give a detailed theology of the diaconate.[7] However, when the biblical material is taken into

7. See Timothy Keller, *Ministries of Mercy: The Call of the Jericho Road* (Grand Rapids: Zondervan, 1989); and Alexander Strauch, *The New Testament Deacon: The Church's Minister of Mercy* (Littleton, CO: Lewis and Roth, 1992).

consideration, it is clear that a distinction can be made between the work of the elders and the work of deacons. Broadly stated, the elder is responsible for the overall spiritual oversight of the flock, while the deacons are to be primarily concerned with the physical and material concerns of the flock. The offices of elders and deacons *together* represent the comprehensive care Christ has provided for his flock.

Unfortunately, as with the office of elder, those who serve as deacons often misunderstand their roles, as do the congregations they serve. In many congregations, deacons are viewed merely as glorified janitors who make sure the building is kept clean and the heat is turned on. While these "physical" needs of the congregation are important, the work of the deacons should also have its focus on the well-being of the individual sheep. The importance of this ministry can be seen in Acts 6, where the foundation is laid for what would eventually become the diaconate.

A serious problem came up when "a complaint arose on the part of the Hellenistic Jews against the native Hebrews, because their widows were being overlooked in the daily serving of food" (Acts 6:1). This was a serious problem. The church was in crisis of being split through favoritism of one group over another. Would the church's survival be jeopardized in its nascent state through prejudice and faction over food? The apostles understood that this needed to be addressed decisively. The gravity of the problem could be seen by the kind of men they sought to solve the challenge. "Therefore, brethren, select from among you seven men of good reputation, full of the Spirit and of wisdom, whom we may put in charge of this task" (Acts 6:3). The challenge of meeting this thorny problem related to the physical needs of the widows of the church required men who were recognized as godly by the congregation. You will note that these individuals were to focus on the physical needs of the congregation.

Most agree that this establishes a perpetual office with the same focus. The apostles saw this need in order that they would be freed from these concerns to devote themselves "to prayer and to the ministry of the word" (Acts 6:4). The ongoing offices of elder and deacon reflect this division of service for the benefit of the flock. The importance of the office of deacon and the wisdom required is apparent in not only the qualifications identified in Acts 6 but also in 1 Timothy 3:8–13, where they are virtually identical to the qualifications for elder, except that elders are to be "able to teach" (1 Tim. 3:2).

With this background in mind, understanding that deacons are an integral part of the care Christ has provided for his flock, they should work together with the elders[8] in providing care for the flock, with responsibility for and expertise in caring for the physical needs of the membership. As you can see, there is a *macro* realm of responsibility for deacons as they care for the overall physical concerns of the congregation (such as building and budget responsibilities). There is also a *micro* area of responsibility as deacons assist the elders by overseeing the physical needs of the individual members of the church. It is for this reason that it is desirable to include deacons with the elders in partnership to shepherd the flock. This idea is not new; David Dickson, nineteenth-century Scotsman, remarked that "the elder should often be in communication with the deacon in his district,

---

8. In many Baptist, independent, and congregational churches, those who provide primary spiritual oversight are termed "deacons." For the benefit of clarifying the biblical offices and roles, it is important that the appropriate biblical nomenclature be adopted. In the Bible, those who provide primary spiritual oversight are called "overseers" or "elders."

advising with him as to persons requiring assistance . . . "[9] The ultimate responsibility rests with the elders, but the deacons fulfill an important biblical role for the well-being of the sheep.

What better way to partner with the deacons in caring for the flock than actually including them on shepherding teams? There are several immediate benefits that come to mind. Firstly, the flock will be getting the comprehensive care designed by the Chief Shepherd in the establishment of these two perpetual offices. Secondly, the congregation will have a proper view of the importance and focus of the work of the deacons. The deacons will no longer be viewed merely as mop pushers and maintenance men but men with responsibility for the care of the physical needs of the flock as well. Thirdly, the deacons themselves will have a proper view of the importance and focus of their work. Fourthly, the elders and deacons will develop an important camaraderie as they work together for the benefit of their respective sheep. In many churches it is rare that the elders and deacons meet together. It might be that they only meet *together* once a year at budget time. What about the working relationship between the elders and deacons in your church? In many churches there is tension between elders and deacons as they tangle over assets or areas of responsibility. Working together on shepherding teams will require more frequent meetings together (as we will see in the "accountability" essential). This helps to build better communication, mutual respect, and trust among the officers as they carry out this work. Finally, this partnership reminds not only the elders but the deacons that their calling is to serve the Lord by serving the sheep for his glory.

The Lord has blessed his church with the offices of elder and deacon. They complement one another and together comprise

9. David Dickson, *The Elder and His Work* (repr., Dallas: Presbyterian Heritage Publications, 1990), 75.

the comprehensive picture of the care that he has designed for his flock. Ideally, shepherding teams should consist of at least one elder and one deacon.

Other Uses of the Flock System

Over the course of time you will find that there are many other advantages of having divided your flock into smaller units under the care of the elders. Here are some suggestions.

Prayer or Email Chains. The smaller units overseen by each elder serve as natural starting points for important communications from church leaders to the congregation. Elders can also contact their groups when matters of significance to their own smaller flocks need to be communicated, without necessarily contacting the entire church.

Congregational Care. In many churches, the entire congregation is contacted to provide support for members who are in need for one reason or another. One example is the practice of many congregations to supply meals for a family just blessed with the arrival of a new baby. Consider using each flock to care for the respective needs of their members. If the need is greater than is manageable by the smaller flock, then move to mobilize another flock or the whole church. Ideally, deacons of that respective flock should coordinate this kind of care, and the deacons should then engage others to assist in coordinating the tasks at hand. This could also include care for the shut-ins or infirm in the respective flock.

Congregational Functions. Many churches continually struggle to find a way to delegate various responsibilities for important

212

church functions. In a recent outreach at our church, there were several important responsibilities that needed to be addressed *every* week for ten weeks. The leaders of the event decided to rotate the various responsibilities (setup, cleanup, greeters, nursery, etc.) through the various flocks. This was a very effective approach to organize the work.

Undoubtedly, there are many other ways that these small flocks can be mobilized for their own health and for the efficient functioning of the church as a whole. Keep your eyes open for such opportunities.

ACTION PLAN

1. What have you done to establish the mutual knowledge between the elders and the flock? Do your members know who "their elder" is? Do the elders know for which specific sheep they are responsible?
2. After you have clarified the membership roll, set aside a meeting for the elders to "draft" the members by family unit using the form provided in appendix A.
3. Consider adding deacons in partnership with the elders as teams to shepherd their sheep.

5. An Effective Shepherding Ministry Must Include the Four Shepherding Functions

If the basic responsibilities of shepherds have been captured by the categories of knowing, feeding, leading, and protecting, an effective shepherding ministry will have to be concerned to address all four of them both on the micro and the macro level.

The primary concern of this book is the micro, relational, personal interaction of leaders with their sheep. This is where most leaders fall short. Referring to the detailed exposition of the four shepherding functions in part 2 of this book, use the questions below to review and assess your shepherding ministry in the four *micro* categories.

ACTION PLAN

1. Micro-knowing: After having delegated the flock, decide what you are going to *do* to develop the relationship with the flock. Are you going to develop a plan of visitation? Are you going to make a commitment to contact members by phone?

2. Micro-feeding: How are you going to approach the ministry of the Word in your contacts with your sheep? Will you take a proactive approach with a Bible study or catechism, or will you simply make yourself available to address questions as they come up in your shepherding contacts?

3. Micro-leading: Can you say, together with the apostle Paul, "Follow me as I follow Christ?" In what areas of your life do you see a need for improvement? Is your personal walk with the Lord a good example to follow? Is your family life a good example for other families in the church? Are you faithful in fulfilling the regular commitments of a church member (tithing, presence at worship, involvement in ministry)?

4. Micro-protection: Do know your sheep well enough to know the challenges and struggles that they face? Set up a system of overseeing member attendance in order to identify when there is a change in attendance pattern. This will enable you to be in a position to respond promptly to such a change.

6. An Effective Shepherding Plan Must Include Accountability

One of the greatest hindrances to the success of most shepherding ministries is the failure of elders to hold one another accountable to accomplish this work. It is one thing to establish and set a plan in motion. It is another thing to make sure that the contacts are being made. If this is a priority of ministry among the elders, there should be regular accountability at least on a monthly basis for making shepherding contacts.

Monthly Accountability

The monthly elders meeting should begin with a period of time (thirty to sixty minutes) to meet in shepherding teams to review the contacts made with the sheep during the previous month. This is an important accountability element as each elder is responsible to report his contacts with each of his assigned sheep. Time should also be spent together praying for the concerns identified. At this meeting the shepherding team should also review the latest attendance review sheets.[10] Each team should

10. See the "Shepherd's View" sheet in appendix A.

also be provided with a form to report the number of successful contacts. This form can also provide opportunity to report other useful information such as change of address, phone number, or other data to the church office.[11]

Ideally, you will have included the deacons on your shepherding teams, and they will join in reporting and in prayer. During these strategic shepherding gatherings, the team may well agree that a particular member needs further attention or care. This demonstrates the consultative benefit of working in teams.

After the time has elapsed for meeting in shepherding teams, the officers should gather together as a whole. This is the time to allow opportunity for teams to inform the whole group if a situation has arisen among their flocks that requires the attention of the entire body. For example, there may be times when a family encounters a crisis that will require the resources of the larger church body to relieve.

If the deacons are involved in the shepherding teams, it is important to meet *together* as officers at least for the purpose of meeting in shepherding teams. However, after the shepherding teams meet, the deacons and elders could meet together for a few minutes to review other matters (financial reports, property concerns, etc.) that may be of interest and concern to all officers in their respective roles.

Finally, after this joint meeting, the deacons and elders should have separate meetings to discuss their particular areas of responsibility and oversight.

In our church, this approach has revolutionized not only the relationship of the officers with the sheep, but also among the officers themselves. The partnership of elders and deacons in caring for the flock has reminded them of their primary

11. See appendix A for a sample report form, or for downloadable forms go to www.theshepherdleader.com.

responsibility before the Lord. Working together has built trust and mutual respect for the God-given responsibilities distinctive to each office and has also increased effectiveness in caring for the flock together. The officers understand that "it's about the sheep."

Whatever shepherding approach is chosen, it is essential that there be regular accountability for contacting the sheep. Unfortunately, if there is no accountability it is unlikely that the shepherding contacts will be completed. Regular accountability not only encourages the elders to contact the sheep but also develops the partnership of the officers in caring for the flock.

Annual Diagnosis

At least on an annual basis, a diagnosis of the status of each member should be completed. This should be compared with the initial diagnosis, which should lead to a clear picture not only of the "health" of individual sheep but of the flock as a whole. It will also indicate what progress, or lack thereof, has been made in the improvement of the health of the flock since the previous evaluation. Ask questions such as: How many members have been reclaimed from "stray" status? How many moved from "weak" to "healthy" status?

Another important consideration at least on an annual basis is the status of chronically "stray" and "lost" sheep. Earlier, the importance of maintaining an accurate membership roll was discussed. "Lost" sheep are those members who are no longer present in *any* way in the worship and life of the church. Their only relationship to the church is that their name appears on the official membership roll. If shepherd-elders have been diligent in their contact and care for the flock, it should be a rare occurrence that a member slips away into this category. However, it *will* happen and, undoubtedly, when a church institutes a shepherding plan and you give attention to the membership roll, you will discover exactly how many people fall into this category.

The annual review assumes that you have made efforts throughout the year to reach these members and that they have failed to respond or are completely resistant to reinvolvement in the worship and life of the church. When most leaders are asked how they deal with inactive members who are unresponsive to their efforts, the leaders respond that those members are "dropped from the roll" of the church. In some cases this is done with deliberate shepherding contact and care, while in other cases it is done with little or no contact with the member, with little or no effort to seek the lost sheep.

It is alarming to note some of the motives mentioned for "keeping the rolls clean." One elder mentioned the following rationale:

> There is a price per communicant member the church must pay to the denomination. If a communicant member is no longer attending, he or she is still paid for. The church must reactivate that member through one of the methods above or remove him so that the church will no longer be obligated to pay the denomination for that member.

While this perspective shows great commitment to the denomination's "askings," it belies an impersonal attitude toward the stray member. Another elder reported, "Keeping the roster accurate is very important for this small church because they need a quorum in voting situations and inactive members would greatly impede this process."

While these comments accurately represent certain administrative dilemmas, it is disturbing when these matters are raised as important issues in relationship to the care of the flock. This isn't shepherding, it's bean counting!

As discussed earlier, the church's membership roll is an important, though imperfect, reflection of those who have been identified as Christ's sheep, those who have heard his voice. Great care must be taken in "removing" them from that list. Such removal is a mere bookkeeping matter in many churches, but in reality is a reflection of the authoritative evaluation of the standing of its members before the Lord. The member dropped from the roll is not merely no longer recognized as a member of that particular church, but is no longer recognized as a member of the *visible* church of Jesus Christ. Therefore, this matter must be pursued with utmost gravity and solemnity and must be bathed in prayer. If, indeed, a member must be removed from the rolls of a church, it must be undertaken with the kind of care the Good Shepherd himself would provide. In some cases, where the reason for absence is sin, appropriate discipline must be pursued with the hope of reclaiming the member not only to the church, but to Christ.

In conclusion, any shepherding plan must provide opportunity for the elders to discuss the well-being of their flock and respond to any needs that arise, *and* the plan must include accountability for completing the contacts. The "business" of the shepherd-elder is the sheep! Working as shepherding teams and reporting to one another encourages completion of the contacts through "peer pressure." When the officer knows that he will be called upon to report on his sheep in the team setting, he will be more likely to complete the contacts. Since the shepherd-elder will be accountable to the Chief Shepherd one day, accountability and encouragement are necessary now to accomplish the care of the flock.

ACTION PLAN

1. If you currently have a shepherding ministry, how do you hold one another accountable for completing the contacts?
2. Consider setting aside the first portion of your monthly officers' meeting to report on shepherding contacts and pray for the sheep.
3. Remember to review the status of "stray" and "lost" sheep with relationship to the church roll at least annually.

7. An Effective Shepherding Plan Must Include Prayer

The work of shepherding is a spiritual endeavor. As such, we are completely dependent on the Lord for his direction and blessing on the work. Hopefully, you will have noticed that the foundation of the comprehensive matrix of shepherding in chapter five is the ministry of the Word and prayer. Effectiveness in every aspect of shepherding (knowing, feeding, leading, and protecting) requires the work of the Spirit in the hearts of shepherds and sheep alike. David Dickson says,

> As elders, individually set to watch over the people committed to us, let us feel that we can do real, lasting good to the souls of our people only so far as the Spirit blesses, and no further. And this blessing is sure, for He is faithful that hath promised, "If ye then, being evil, know how to give good gifts unto your children, *how much more* shall your heavenly Father give the Holy Spirit to them that ask him!"[12]

12. Dickson, *The Elder and His Work*, 81.

The Lord has called you to this work. He is eager to bless you as you serve him by serving his sheep. We must then begin by asking him for wisdom to carry out this task, realizing that we can accomplish nothing of lasting value apart from him. Samuel Miller commended prayer to elders who truly sensed their own inadequacy to shepherd the flock:

> The deeper his own sense of his own unfitness, the more likely will he be to apply unceasingly and opportunately for heavenly aid; and the nearer he lives to the throne of grace, the more largely he will partake of that wisdom and strength which he needs.[13]

It is sad to consider how much of the work of the Lord is carried out in our own strength, without seeking the Lord's blessing. As leaders we are often called upon to lead the congregation in prayer publicly, but is our private prayer life as vital as it should be? Jonathan Edwards wrote two sermons entitled "Hypocrites Deficient in the Duty of Prayer." In the second sermon he makes this convicting challenge:

> He that prays only when he prays with others, would not pray at all, were it not that the eyes of others are upon him. He that will not pray where none but God see him, manifestly doth not pray at all out of respect for God, or regard to his all-seeing eye, and therefore doth in effect cast off prayer.[14]

We must be leaders who are qualified to lead not merely in public prayer, but whose private prayer lives would also be exemplary to those who are called to follow us as we follow Christ.

13. Samuel Miller, *The Ruling Elder* (1832; repr., Dallas, TX: Presbyterian Heritage Publications, 1999), 264.

14. Jonathan Edwards, *The Works of Jonathan Edwards* (Carlisle, PA: Banner of Truth, 1979), 2:75.

In addition to the elements of prayer that every believer should practice, the shepherd-elder has the responsibility and privilege of praying for the needs of his little flock. In the regular monthly contacts with the sheep, prayer requests should be sought and written down. The caring shepherd will not merely be satisfied to hear these requests, but he will regularly carry them to the throne of grace in his personal prayer time. These requests will then provide a natural place to pick up in the next shepherding contact. However, follow-up on these concerns should not always wait until the next "official" contact. The elder should be eager to follow up as soon as possible to see how things are progressing. The elder may also follow up with counsel, consultation, or other resources, depending on the need.

In addition to praying privately for the sheep, the elder will bring these requests to the monthly meeting with the other officers on his shepherding team. This sharing of requests not only serves as a means of accountability but as another layer of intercession for the sheep. In this caring partnership, depending on the requests, the officers should prayerfully consider ways that the prayer concerns might be addressed.

Prayer is urgently needed for those who are stray or lost sheep. What will change their hearts? What moves the prodigal to want to return home? *Pray* that the Spirit of the Lord will convict them and open their hearts to hear the voice of the Good Shepherd calling them back to the fold. Our elders recently set apart another dedicated time of prayer (on the fifth Monday) to pray just for stray and lost sheep. This is in addition to the regular stated monthly meetings in which shepherding teams meet to pray for the sheep. All of our prayer times should demonstrate our complete dependence on the Lord to accomplish what we alone cannot.

Elders should also make their flocks aware that they are willing to come and pray personally with them when requested to do so. The words of James remind the flock to call for the elders when they are sick: "Is anyone among you sick? Then he must call for the elders of the church and they are to pray over him, anointing him with oil in the name of the Lord" (James 5:14). The members of the church should know that their elders care and are willing to come to them. Shepherd-elders, therefore, pray not only *for* the sheep, but *with* the sheep.

Many shepherding plans have the other six elements in place, but fail to give careful attention to the matter of prayer. Effectiveness in shepherding is only possible when elders are faithful in prayer. Faithfulness in private prayer for the sheep will only happen when elders are convinced that they can only succeed with God's blessing. The great Scottish pastor Thomas Chalmers sought to impress his elders with the need to look to the Lord for fruitfulness in their work. He addressed these words to the elders of St. John's Church as he first set them apart for their shepherding ministry:

> We are apt to confide in the efficacy and wisdom of our own arrangements—to set up a framework of skillful contrivance, and think that so good an apparatus will surely be productive of something . . . that on the strength of elderships and deaconships . . . some great and immediate effect is to follow. God will put to shame the proud confidence of man in the efficacy of his own wisdom, and He will have all the glory of all the spiritual good that is done in the world and your piety will, therefore, work a tenfold mightier effect than your talents, in the cause you have undertaken; and your pains without your prayers will positively do nothing in this way, though it must be confessed that prayers without pains are just as unproductive,

and that because they must be prayers of insincerity [without the pains] as can not rise with acceptance to heaven. It is the union of both which best promises an apostolical effect to your truly apostolical office; and with these few simple remarks do I commend you to Him who alone can bless you in this laudable undertaking, and give comfort and efficacy to the various duties that are involved with it.[15]

ACTION PLAN

1. Do you pray for your individual sheep and their needs on a regular basis?
2. What will you do to build prayer for the flock into your private prayer lives and into your gathering as leaders?

---

15. Hanna, ed., *Memoirs of the Life and Writings of Thomas Chalmer* (New York: Harper and Brothers, 1850), 2:301.

IMPLICATIONS OF HAVING A SHEPHERDING MINISTRY

IF THE CALLING to shepherd the flock is taken seriously, it will have several important implications in our approach to ministry.

Implications for Potential Elders

If the primary responsibility of the elder is to shepherd the flock, this has enormous implications for the qualifications, training, and selection of elders.

Qualifications

When congregations are in need of elders, what do they look for? Unfortunately, many don't know *what* to look for! In many churches, members assume that because an individual has been successful in business or financially, that they are qualified to be an elder. Undoubtedly, this is the reason that so many church boards are filled with men with a "board of directors" mentality. I am not saying this because a person who is successful financially or in business is *not* qualified to serve. In fact, these accomplishments are gifts from God, but in and of themselves, they do not qualify a man to serve in the office of elder. What, then, *should* we look for in a prospective elder?

Firstly, the character qualifications in 1 Timothy 3:1–7 and Titus 1:5–9 should be foremost in considering prospective elders. If elders are to be "examples to the flock," this is where that example must begin. Obviously, no one meets these qualifications perfectly, but there must be no blatant exceptions to these standards. While no one is perfect, the power of the work of the gospel in the elder's life must be such that he is "above reproach," Paul's first qualification (1 Tim. 3:2).

Secondly, if elders are shepherds, another qualification must be a demonstrated love for the sheep and a willingness to take part in the shepherding ministry of the elders. When the time comes for the nomination of elders (either by a committee or the congregation, depending on the church's structure), the character qualifications and "aptitude" for shepherding should be at the forefront. There should be clear evidence that the individual has already been active in serving the flock corporately and personally. These biblical qualifications should be communicated to the congregation as the process is begun through public announcement and carefully prepared documents describing the process.

Training

It's hard to believe, but some churches provide very little training for the office of elder. Sadly, in settings where there is training, very little attention is given to the important ministry of shepherding the flock. Ask yourself the question, "What do we include in officer training?" In many settings, particularly in reformed and Presbyterian congregations, elder training consists almost exclusively of a study of the doctrinal standards of the church. There is no doubt that this is a crucial aspect of training since elders must sincerely believe these truths and be prepared to teach and defend them. However, doctrinal orientation should only be part of the process of elder training. A holistic framework for leadership training must be kept in mind.[1]

Since the biblical character qualifications are so clearly identified, it is very important to study and discuss them with every elder candidate.[2] Candidates should have an opportunity to assess themselves with regard to these qualifications and to disqualify themselves if the Lord convicts them that there is an area (or areas) in which there is a significant deficiency. Such a disqualification should be discussed in consultation with the pastor and the current elders.

In addition to doctrinal orientation and character qualifications, prospective candidates should be oriented to the shepherding responsibilities he will assume as an elder. This should not be a surprise to him since he has been part of a flock as an active member and has benefited from the ministry of his elder-shepherd. In any case, it must be clear that to be an elder is to be a shepherd and that he will be expected to take part. In fact, if the candidate is subsequently approved to serve as an elder, it is best to partner him with the shepherding team who provided

1. Review the "Comprehensive Framework for Leadership Formation" in chapter 7.

2. For a downloadable study of the qualifications for leadership found in 1 Timothy 3:1–7, go to www.theshepherdleader.com.

care for his family up to the point of his election. This will enable him to "apprentice" with an elder and the flock with whom he is already familiar. As the congregation grows and people are added to this flock, this becomes the natural means of multiplying the number of elder-led flocks.

If these qualifications are clear to nominee and congregation alike, and the elder training is effective, the likelihood is small that anyone who is not interested in the shepherding ministry will be elected as an elder of the church.

Implications for Current Elders

What do you do if, in your attempt to implement a shepherding plan, a current elder or two are reluctant to participate? This is not an unlikely scenario given that many elders "signed on" expecting to be on a board of directors, making decisions for the well-being of the congregation rather than being involved in the sheep-intensive care of the flock.

The wise pastor must realize that not all elders will be equally enthused about ministering to the flock through a shepherding plan that requires them to be in regular contact with members. After instructing them in the scriptural mandate to shepherd the flock, some may still be reluctant. At Crossroads, after the shepherding effort had been underway for some time, one longtime elder admitted to me that he had made none of his calls and had no interest in doing so. These circumstances revealed yet another advantage of the "shepherding team" concept. We merely "grandfathered" this non-shepherding elder (an oxymoron) into a shepherding team with another "shepherding" elder (and two deacons) who were willing to make contacts. He sat with the shepherding team at monthly meetings while reports from contacts were given and prayers for the needs of the sheep were offered. The hope was that he would grow interested in making a few contacts as he saw the excitement of the other men and the congregation for the shepherding ministry. What happened? He moved away before he was able to be won over to the importance of this shepherding role.

In any case, it is important to be patient with these elders, to pray that the Lord will bring them along as partners in this effort. However, I would go as far to say that an elder who refuses to take *any part* in the shepherding ministry should give serious consideration as to whether he is truly qualified to serve in this office. Shepherding is not a matter of "gifting" or "preference," but shepherding is at the heart of the calling and identity of the office of elder and, therefore, is a *sine qua non* of service.

Implications for the "Class" System or "Term" Eldership

This brings us to another important consideration: the class system. The class system of office in the church is also known as the "rotating officer" or "term" system (used synonymously here). For example, elders elected become part of a class. Depending on the length of term, each year has a "class" of elders who are elected, say, in 2009. If the term is three years, these elders would be in the "class of 2012." This identifies how long they will serve as "active" elders (three years) and when their "term" of service ends (2012).

This system is contrary to the nature and function of the office of elder, both biblically and practically.[3] Biblically speaking, there is no warrant for terms in office. While the advisability of an occasional sabbatical from active service is arguable, it is not consonant with the manner in which the class system functions in many churches.

Practically speaking, when asked about the advantage of term eldership, the most common answer is that "it enables us to rotate 'bad' elders off every three years." What a noble motive for embracing a structure to guide church government! Of course, the problem is that you also rotate the *good* elders off every three years as well. (By the way, no churches of which I am aware have terms for teaching elders!)

Another problem is that, in most cases, term eldership is based on an artificial number of "spots" that must be filled. In most churches where this system has been adopted, each class contains, for example, three spots. When that class has concluded its service, it is incumbent upon the congregation to fill those spots, whether or not there are qualified individuals to fill those positions. This often leads to individuals being pushed forward who may not have the calling, gifts, or desire to serve. How should you go about determining the number of elders that your congregation should have? The answer is that only the men who are gifted, called, and qualified should serve in the offices of the church. This is the number of elders your church should have. No more. No less.

A fundamental problem with term eldership is in the matter of shepherding. Rotating elders on and off can disrupt the

3. I am in full agreement with John Murray on this point and am indebted to his treatment of the subject. See John Murray, *Collected Writings* (Carlisle, PA: Banner of Truth, 1977), 2:351–56, reproduced in appendix B with permission.

continuity of shepherding care. Elders may just have gained the trust of their sheep, and then they rotate off the active service roster. If your church has term eldership, consider this suggestion for the sake of shepherding continuity. If an elder's "active" term is completed, relieve him of some of the macro duties of service, such as committee responsibilities and even the "business" portion of the officers' meeting. However, keep him on his shepherding team with continuing responsibility to contact his sheep, report on the contacts, and pray for the sheep. The number of his required contacts may even be diminished somewhat, but his ongoing service as a shepherd among the flock is what God has called upon him to do.

The better option would be to eliminate term eldership altogether. As Murray says, "There is no sound practical argument [for term eldership] that cannot be offset by a multiplicity of practical arguments on the other side."[4]

Implications for Member Orientation

Most churches have a class designed to introduce prospective members to the distinctives of that local church. These classes vary in length from church to church, but they ordinarily provide an overview of the beliefs, practices, procedures, and distinctives of the church.

It is very important in this process to provide prospective members with an introduction to the shepherding ministry of the church. They should be given an overview of the *purpose* of the shepherding ministry of the elders, demonstrating its

4. Ibid., 2:356.

biblical foundation. They should also be introduced to the *plan* in place in your church. Tell them exactly what they can expect. Tell them that the elders are eager to minister to them and to pray for them. Also tell them that the information and prayer requests gleaned through elder contacts will be handled discreetly. Most Christians will be greatly encouraged to know that their elders are going to take their responsibility seriously to provide spiritual care for them and their families.

The biblical metaphor of shepherding also provides a context to introduce prospective members to some subjects that are more sensitive. For example, many people have not been in a church where the matter of church discipline is taken seriously. However, if they are going to commit themselves to "submit to the government and discipline of the church,"[5] they need to have a basic understanding of what that actually means. Unfortunately, in some cases this part of the member orientation, if it is included at all, relies on a passing reference to the denominational "book of discipline" as its text. There may well be a place for immersion into the details of the process and procedures of discipline as outlined in these tomes, but this is probably not the place to start.

Instead, an introduction to the shepherding ministry of the elders provides a natural opportunity to introduce new members to the elders' important responsibility to "protect" the flock through discipline. The elders of the church are committed to "seek" after those who stray. New members need to know the meaning of submitting to the discipline of the church. Quite simply, it means that if they stray (in doctrine or practice), the

5. These are the words used in the membership vows of the Presbyterian Church in America.

elders in this church will take seriously their responsibility to seek them and restore them.

Provide new members with a basic orientation to Matthew 18:15–20 *in context*. Remind them that this foundational passage for church discipline is immediately preceded in the text by the story of the good shepherd who leaves the ninety-nine to seek after the one lost sheep (18:12–14). The process of going individually, then taking another along, and finally "telling it to the church" is the practical implementation of the story of seeking the lost sheep. Both accounts make clear that the purpose of seeking the lost sheep is not punitive, but restorative. This is also apparent in the parable that immediately follows (18:21–35). Jesus told the parable to answer Peter's question, "Lord, how often shall my brother sin against me and I forgive him? Up to seven times?" (v. 21). Peter's thought was that he was being extremely generous, but the parable that Jesus told challenges us to forgive graciously as a reflection of the forgiveness that we have received from the Father through faith in Jesus Christ.

You can see how Matthew 18 places discipline in a context immediately following verses that present a shepherd eager to seek for the lost and immediately before a text that teaches the urgency of forgiveness. This provides a holistic picture of the shepherd's ministry to watch, seek, restore, and forgive. What a wonderful way to give prospective members the big picture of the responsibility of the elders of the church to protect the flock in this way. Hopefully, putting this important shepherding responsibility in its biblical context will lay the proper foundation for seeking strays when the need arises.

One final suggestion for the new member process. In many churches it is customary to bring new members forward in order to introduce them to the congregation. In many cases the new members are asked to affirm certain commitments as members of the church, including a commitment to "submit to the government and discipline of the church." Essentially, in this commitment they are saying, "Yes, I submit to your authority as a shepherd-elder to provide care and direction for my life in Christ." At Crossroads, we have found it helpful to add another question in this setting. Instead of another affirmation from the new member, it is an affirmation *from the shepherd-elders* of the church. As the new member candidates are standing, ask the elders of the church to stand and ask them to affirm the following commitment: "Will you as undershepherds of this congregation undertake the responsibility of shepherding these new members who have now placed themselves under your care?" As they say, "We will!" there is a visible and audible reminder to the congregation *and* to the elders of this important relationship between the sheep and their elders.

Implications for Church Discipline

In addition to the comments already made about the importance of the work of discipline for shepherds of the church, having a delegated flock is a great aid in the *implementation* of church discipline. This came to my attention recently as a serious problem arose with one of the members of our church. One of the officers in the flock contacted me and indicated that the shepherding team thought that it would be good to meet with me to discuss the matter. When I got back to them to try to set up the meeting, they reported that the officers of their flock had already addressed the matter! What a wonderful testimony to the competence and care of these elders and deacons that they took the initiative to reach out to this stray sheep. When issues go beyond the first (one on one) and second (take another with you) approaches of Matthew 18, the officers in a particular flock can serve as the first level of the "tell it to the church" stage. Hopefully, the relationships established through regular shepherding contacts and care will have provided a credibility in the eyes of the sheep that will move them to take the matter seriously as the officers try to reclaim them. If this fails, then they can bring the matter before the larger body of elders for their attention.[6]

Who Shepherds the Shepherds?

A question that often comes to mind is, "Who shepherds the shepherds?" As the elders are busy doing the work of contacting and caring for the sheep, who contacts and cares for *them*? First of all, if there are deacons on the shepherding teams, the elders should take responsibility to care for them and their families as they do for the other members in their flock. Concerning the shepherding care for the elders, a good approach is to have the pastor or someone on the pastoral staff contact and provide care for them. In most cases this is a manageable load for the pastor to handle. If there are a large number of elders, this responsibility can be shared by other members of the pastoral staff.

6. In matters of church discipline it is very important for officers to follow denominational procedures as closely as possible. Sadly, this is necessary not only to guide the officers and protect the rights of the church member, but to protect the church in this litigious age.

The next logical question is, "Who cares for the pastor?" This can get complicated. Probably the best answer is to encourage the elders as a whole (or to delegate to one or two), to provide contact and concern for the pastor and his family. It is true that pastoral ministry can be a very lonely calling. Think how beneficial it would be for pastors to receive regular inquiry as to the well-being and the health of their families. This is attention that pastors need like anyone else. Unfortunately, just like with the sheep, the only time many pastors hear from their elders is when there is a problem or a need to be met. Take the time to provide proactive contact and care for your pastoral staff as well.

Implications for Other Ministries within the Church

Many have found it helpful for ministries within the church to employ a similar shepherding approach. For example, some youth ministers and college ministers have made commitments to maintain regular shepherding contact with the individuals within the scope of their areas of responsibility. They have sought to do this not only with active members of their ministries but with those who may be merely "prospects." This is particularly important in the college years since this is the time when people tend to drift away from the church.

When ministries within the church begin to shepherd those in their groups, it merely reinforces the care of the church by providing multiple layers of care and concern for members and prospects alike.

Implications for Church Planting

When most people think about church planting they think about strategies for winning people to Christ. When this happens, the church will grow. Reaching people for Christ is a mission with which *every* church should be engaged. For the church planter, however, there is a sense of "do or die" attached to it.

Yet church planters should not let themselves focus on those outside the church while failing to shepherd those already in the church. People come in the front door and move out the back door just as quickly in church plants as in established churches. In church plants in particular, the novelty and excitement of being part of something "new" wears off, or people are put off by the hard work required of *every* member in a church plant. In any case, it is urgent that church planters make a commitment to establish the ministry of shepherding among a new congregation as soon as possible. The benefits of care and communication between shepherd and sheep are absolutely vital to the church planter. Don't be so concerned with the "outward" face of the church that you neglect the "inward" face of congregational care.

As a church planter, you may have to bear the responsibilities of shepherding care alone at first. As soon as you begin to train potential elders to work alongside you, be sure to introduce them to the biblical responsibilities of the elder as shepherd. In church planting situations it can be very encouraging when an elder from another church comes alongside you in the work. However, don't be too quick to "lay hands" on these men unless you have confirmed that they have a "shepherding" view of the office of elder. A thorough qualification and training period for elder candidates in the new church should help you determine who among them has a shepherd's heart. These men will be the foundation of your ministry. Don't compromise or settle for anything less than shepherding elders.

An Organic Approach to Church Planting

Another advantage of a well-developed shepherding plan is that it can provide a natural means of developing new churches. This is particularly applicable when there has been a geographically developed "parish" system of elder care in the mother church. Hopefully, each flock will continue to grow, and the elders and deacons in each flock will continue to become more and more competent in their ability to care for the sheep. If your church is serious about planting churches, why not prepare a particular flock in a particular location, as it reaches a particular size, to become a new particular church? Leadership and relationships have been established and a network of caring is already in place. These are essential elements of an effective church plant. Of course, this is more likely to happen when the mother church embraces such a vision from the very outset.

For Further Reflection

Implications for Potential Elders

1. Does the basis for elder nomination in your church include the character qualifications of 1 Timothy 3 and Titus 1? Does it include the importance of the shepherding "aptitude" of nominees? Are these communicated to your members *and* potential nominees?

2. Does your officer training include the biblical character qualifications and introduction to the importance of shepherding?

Implications for the "Class" System or "Term" Eldership

3. Does your church employ "term eldership"? Be honest—do you really think it is biblical? Discuss the implications of this structure for "shepherding" elders. What would be necessary for you to move away from this system?

4. If you plan to continue term eldership, how will you assure continuity in the shepherding ministry of your church? Consider continuing to use "inactive" elders in the shepherding ministry even if they are released from other responsibilities.

Implications for Member Orientation

5. Do you include an introduction to the shepherding ministry of the elders in your new member orientation?

6. Consider the appropriate place to introduce this material in the context of what you already present to prospective members.

Who Shepherds the Shepherds?

7. Decide who will take responsibility for shepherding the elders. Will it be the teaching elder?

8. Decide who will take responsibility to care for the pastor and his family. Will it be an elder or group of elders? Will it be another staff person?

Implications for Other Ministries within the Church

9. Are there other ministries that could benefit by putting together a shepherding strategy for member care?

10. Provide a training time for ministry leaders to introduce them to these shepherding principles.

Implications for Church Planting

11. Do you have a plan to shepherd the flock immediately in the new plant?
12. Put into place a proactive shepherding plan so that those who join you will be well cared for from the outset.
13. When seeking your first elder candidates, be sure to search for those who will fulfill the biblical role of shepherd and include this material in your officer training.

II

LET'S GET STARTED! SUGGESTIONS FOR IMPLEMENTATION

YOU MIGHT BE wondering exactly how to get a shepherding ministry started. This brief chapter contains an overview with some practical suggestions to introduce a shepherding ministry at your church. Many of these suggestions are built on the foundation of the material covered earlier but will seek to concentrate them into a simplified format. For even more practical insight, visit the companion website to this book, www.theshepherdleader.com.

Ten Steps for Elders to Implement a Shepherding Ministry

1. Study the biblical foundations for the work of shepherding provided in chapters 1 and 2.

2. Spend time doing a general analysis of how well the leadership team is doing in addressing the macro- and micro-shepherding functions outlined in part 2. Where are the strengths? Where are the weaknesses?

3. Study the seven essential elements of an effective shepherding ministry outlined in chapter 8 in order to assess an existing plan or to develop a new plan.

4. Form into shepherding teams (using elders and deacons where applicable). Teams should have at least two officers for the purpose of accountability. Prayerfully commit yourselves together to shepherd the flock entrusted to you by the Good Shepherd and to hold one another accountable to complete the work.

5. Spend time clarifying the membership roll in order that you will know for which sheep your leadership team is accountable. As you do this, remember to complete the initial diagnosis of the sheep.

6. Delegate the members among the shepherding teams using the "elder draft" method if possible. Remember to take into account natural connections that exist between elders and members. Remember not to put too many "stray" or "lost" sheep with a single team. Don't forget to include the "circumstantially inactive" members (those at college, in ministry, shut-ins, moved away, etc.) as you delegate the sheep. If you are interested in developing a church-planting strategy, consider taking geographical concerns into account as you delegate the sheep so that local groups can later be spun off into new churches.

7. Determine how you will go about making the important relational contacts with the sheep. Will you contact members monthly by phone? Will you visit them in their homes

annually? Will you use a combination of the above or some other strategy? Be sure to plan to make contacts with sufficient frequency so as to nurture the relationship.

8. Commit to hold one another accountable for making personal contact with the sheep. Set aside the first part of each monthly meeting (or plan a separate meeting) to meet in shepherding teams in order to report on contacts made and to pray for the requests secured from the members.

9. Decide on a means of overseeing the attendance of members in worship and involvement in ministry. Will you use a "shepherd's view" master attendance roster updated by pastoral staff from week to week? Will you use pew pads or bulletin tear-offs to monitor member attendance? Be sure to decide on a method that includes the step of providing the information to the elders.

10. Begin making shepherding contacts only after the following congregational steps are taken.

Four Steps to Prepare the Congregation

1. After, and only after, the leadership has developed biblical convictions about shepherding the flock and has settled on a plan, the pastor should preach a *brief series of sermons.* The series should introduce the congregation to the biblical theology of shepherding followed by the importance of the biblical shepherding responsibilities of elders.[1] This might require some corporate repenting

---

1. First Peter 5 or Acts 20 would be a great place to start. Remember to make use of some of the Old Testament foundations as well.

by the elders or led by the pastor on behalf of the elders for a potentially long drought in fulfilling this work. The pastor should then introduce the details of the plan that the elders have agreed to carry out among the sheep. Undoubtedly, the congregation will receive this news with great encouragement as they will now be able to look forward to the personal care of their elders.

2. Soon after the plan is announced, a letter should go out to each family or individual member reiterating the commitment of the elders and the details of the plan agreed upon. This letter should provide each member or family unit with the name of their shepherds. It should not say, "You were *assigned* to elder so-and-so" but "You were *chosen* by elder so-and-so." This more accurately represents the elder draft and also communicates a desire on the part of the elder to care for this particular family.

3. You might want to have an initial "flock party" for the sheep under the care of each particular elder in order to summarize the importance of the shepherding ministry and to answer any questions members might have. This is optional but can be an important step in the process. When it comes to information, more is usually better!

4. Let the sheep know that they don't have to wait for the monthly call in order to contact their elder with prayer requests and concerns.

One Last Thing

As elders you should agree on a date (month) you will begin your shepherding ministry. Any time is good to begin *except* for the summer months when it is less likely that you will be successful in making contacts. You want to be encouraged by starting the ministry at a time when you will have a greater likelihood of success in making the calls or visits.

For the sake of accountability, the starting time (when contacts will begin) should be announced to the congregation in the pastor's sermon series and in the letter that is sent to members. You should do everything that you can to prepare the congregation for the calls they are about to receive in order that they won't be alarmed as they hear personally from their elders! Sheep are "skitterish" and might think the worst unless every effort has been made to inform them of the shepherding strategy. The timing of the congregational information letter is especially important to prepare "stray" and "lost" sheep that they are about to hear from an elder in the church.

After, and only after, these steps have been taken, GET STARTED. It is important during this first month that every effort be made to complete contacts with *every* member. Unfortunately, cynicism and frustration can arise all too quickly when a plan is presented and then not begun in a timely manner. On the other hand, a plan well executed will gain you the appreciation of the members for the effort you are making and also a joyful heart and a clear conscience as you go about the work that the Lord has called you to do.

CONCLUSION

"Like Sheep Without A Shepherd?"

"When I look before me, and consider what, through the blessing of God, this work, if well managed, is like to effect, it makes my heart leap for joy."—Richard Baxter

EVERY FALL SEMESTER I have the opportunity to teach a course at Westminster Seminary entitled "Church Dynamics and Pastoral Practice." In this course I present much of the material that you have read in the pages of this book. In the first class I always ask this question, "Does the church of which you are a member have a shepherding ministry?" It is very sad that rarely are more than three or four hands raised in the entire class. Teaching this material to them has been an encouragement as many of them have sought to apply these principles to the places God has called them to serve.

Now I must ask *you* this question: "Does *your* church have a shepherding ministry?" As Jesus walked through the villages and countryside of Israel and observed the sad condition of the people, he declared that the people were "like sheep without a shepherd." At the conclusion of this book there is only one question left for you to ask: are your church members "like sheep without a shepherd?" I trust that these pages have demonstrated that "shepherding" is not an antiquated, irrelevant metaphor but an urgent need in today's church.

The church desperately needs elders who think like shepherds, not like a board of directors. The church desperately needs elders who love the sheep and are committed to provide not only direction for the congregation as a whole but personal care for its members. I hope you have been convinced that this is the case based on the biblical material presented early in the book. While I have sought to provide practical suggestions for you to apply the biblical principles in your church, each body of elders will need to give prayerful consideration as to how to apply the principles in your context (though the seven essential elements of an effective shepherding plan are nearly non-negotiable!). As J. I. Packer reflected on the shepherding work of Richard Baxter he issued the following challenge:

> How to do this today would have to be worked out in terms of present circumstances, which are very different from those Baxter knew and describes; but Baxter's question to us is, should we not be attempting this, as a practice constantly necessary? If he convinces us that we should, it will not be beyond us to find a method of doing it that suits our situation; where there's a will, there's a way![1]

Are you convinced? If so, you will find a way, hopefully with the help of the principles in this book, to establish a shepherding ministry in your church that will care for your flock.

1. J. I. Packer, introduction to Richard Baxter, *The Reformed Pastor* (1656; repr., Carlisle, PA: Banner of Truth, 1997), 19.

As a church leader the sheep *will* require your attention. It is your choice whether it will be the *reactive* care of running after the troubled and stray sheep or whether it will be time spent *proactively* caring for the sheep in a well-designed shepherding ministry. I hope I have also made the case that time spent in a proactive shepherding plan might not merely help preclude the straying of the sheep but will put you in a better position to respond when there is a problem among the flock. The choice is yours!

Enter the ministry of shepherding with a great sense of joyful expectation. Expect to be encouraged as you see the Good Shepherd at work *in* you as you rely on his grace and wisdom to minister to the flock. Expect to see the Lord at work *through* you as you feed, lead, and protect the sheep for whom he shed his blood. I close with the words used by David Dickson to end his treatise on the subject:

> It is but a few short years any of us will have to do this service for our Lord here below. Let us do it heartily, with all our might, and always as to the Lord. "And when the chief shepherd shall appear, ye shall receive the crown of glory that fadeth not away." (1 Peter 5:4)[2]

2. Dickson, *The Elder and His Work* (repr., Dallas: Presbyterian Heritage Publications, 1990), 82.

APPENDIX A

ADDITIONAL RESOURCES

IN THIS APPENDIX you will find three sample tools to consider as you implement your shepherding plan. These can also be found at www.theshepherdleader.com for free download and editing for your ministry setting.

First is the *Delegating the Flock* tool. After your elders and deacons have formed into shepherding teams, use this tool for the "draft" of members for the various "flocks." List the members by family unit. Remember to use relational connections (e.g., is the family or member in an elder's small group or ministry?). If you are using a geographical approach, make sure that "parishes" with more members have sufficient shepherds to make regular contacts. In any case, do not delegate too many difficult "stray" or "lost" sheep to any team. Do not forget to draft the "circumstantially inactive," including students at college, members in the military or on the mission field, and shut-ins. You will find that the drafting process doesn't take long.

Second is the *Shepherd's View Sheet*. Each shepherding team should have its own shepherd's view sheet in which the team is listed together with the members of their flock. In the first column you will indicate the date of the most recent contact (dedicated shepherding phone call or visit). Next you will see two months of attendance records that should be filled in manually by the "eyeball" approach to keeping track of worship attendance (or whichever means you choose). This is followed by a column in which you should list the ministry with which the member is involved. Remember, this is an important commitment of a member of the church. Finally, there is a column for you to write down the prayer requests you are given when you contact the member. The *Shepherd's View Sheet* should be updated every month for each team.

Third is the *Sample Monthly Shepherding Team Report*. This report is an important accountability element. Each shepherding team should submit the report after their team's monthly accountability meeting. This report indicates the number of contacts made as well as a place for change in member information (phone number, address, etc.), or any comments that need to be communicated.

Delegating the Flock

Elder #1 & Deacon	Elder #2 & Deacon	Elder #3 & Deacon	Elder #4 & Deacon	Elder #5 & Deacon

Shepherd's View Sheet

Elder/Deacon	Last Contact Date	February					March				Ministry	Prayer Request
		1	8	15	22	29	7	14	21	28		
1												
Name												
2												
Name												
3												
Name												
4												
Name												
Shut-In												
Name												
College												
Name												
Moved Away												
Name												

Sample Monthly Shepherding Team Report

Monthly Report Sheet

Shepherding Care Ministry

Month _____

Meeting Date: _____

Team Leader: _____

Contact Success Ratio (Total Possible/Contacts Made):

    Resident Members: _____ / _____

    Shut-in Members: _____ / _____

    Moved Away: _____ / _____

Information (Address/Phone, etc.) Updates:

_____

_____

_____

Comments/Questions:

_____

_____

_____

APPENDIX B

"ARGUMENTS AGAINST TERM ELDERSHIP"

BY JOHN MURRAY[1]

The question being discussed in this brief article is whether ruling elders, in being elected and ordained, may be elected and ordained to the office for a limited and specified period of time, or whether election and ordination should have in view permanent tenure and exercise of the office. The position being taken by the present writer is the latter, namely, that the idea of being ordained to office for a limited period of time is without warrant from the New Testament, and is contrary to the implications of election and ordination. In taking this position, it is necessary at the outset to make clear what it does not involve. It does not mean that a ruling elder may not be removed from office. Of

1. John Murray, *Collected Writings* (Carlisle, PA: Banner of Truth, 1977), 2:351–56. Reproduced with permission of the Banner of Truth Trust.

course an elder may be deposed from office for false doctrine or immorality. And even though he may not be guilty of error or immorality, he may be relieved of his office for other reasons. For example, he may prove to be destitute of the requisite gifts and, in such an event, it would be a travesty of the order instituted by Christ for him to continue to retain the office and presume to exercise its functions. The elder in such a case may resign and his resignation should be accepted. Or he may simply be divested of his office by the proper action of the session. What the procedure would be in this latter case is not our interest at the present time. Again, when an elder ceases to be able to exercise the functions of the office, he should no longer retain the office. This inability may arise from infirmity, or the elder in question may have to move from the locality in which the congregation that elected him resides, so that he is no longer able to discharge the duties. It is not feasible for the elder to retain his office in these circumstances—we may not separate the office from its functions. Ordination to permanent tenure of the office, therefore, does not in the least degree interfere with the duty of resignation from office when that is necessary, nor with the right and duty of removal from office when the circumstances require it. The question in debate is something quite different. It is true that the practice of ordaining ruling elders for a limited period has a long history in Reformed Churches. Many interesting facts could be brought to light if that history were to be traced. But now we are concerned to discover what may be elicited from the Scripture on the question.

In support of the position adopted in this article, it will have to be said, *first of* all, that there is no *overt* warrant from the New Testament for what we may call "term eldership." There is no intimation in the relevant passages that the elders in question were ordained to the office for a specified term. This is a consideration that must not lightly be dismissed. While it does not, of itself, conclusively determine the question, yet it is necessary to take account of this absence of explicit warrant for term eldership. We must bear in mind that there are two ways in which the Scripture reveals to us God's will, namely, what is expressly set down in Scripture, and what by good and necessary consequence may be deduced from Scripture. We are now concerned with the former, and we are affirming at the outset that, in respect of express warrant, there is no evidence to support the idea of term eldership.

It could well be argued, however, that, though there is no express warrant for term eldership, yet there is no evidence against it, and the New Testament leaves the matter an open question; it is a matter on which the New Testament does not legislate. It is this position that the present writer controverts. While the New Testament does not *expressly* legislate against term eldership, there are considerations which fall into the category of good and necessary inference, and which militate against the propriety of this practice. These considerations are derived from the implications which underlie or inhere in the acts of electing and ordaining to this office, implications which are incompatible with the idea of term eldership.

It is quite obvious that the qualifications for eldership are well defined in the New Testament (I Tim. 3:1–7; Titus 1:5–9; cf. Acts 20:28–35). The qualifications are of a high order, and they imply that the person possessing them is endowed with them by the Holy Spirit and by Christ the head of the church. The implication is that the person thus qualified is invested with these gifts and graces to the end that he may serve the church of Christ in that capacity for which these endowments fit him.

There are diversities of gifts in the church of God, and the gifts possessed dictate the function or functions which each person is to perform in the unity of the whole body. Now the gifts for eldership are not of a temporary character. If a person possesses them, the implication is that he permanently possesses them. Sadly enough he may through unfaithfulness lose them. But when a man possesses them we must proceed upon the assumption that he is going to prove faithful, and we may not entertain any suspicion to the effect that he is going to prove unfaithful. The simple fact is that when a man possesses certain endowments which qualify him for eldership, we must proceed on the assumption that they are abiding, and permanently qualify him for the discharge of the functions of the office.

When the congregation elects a man to the office of elder, and when the session ordains him to the office, both the congregation and the session must be convinced that he is possessed of these qualifications. When they act otherwise they violate the New Testament institution. But this judgment on the part of congregation and session involves more than the conviction that he is possessed of these qualifications; it is also judgment to the effect that, by reason of the gifts with which he is endowed, Christ the head of the church, and the Holy Spirit who dwells in the church, are calling this man to the exercise of this sacred office. In other words, the congregation and session ought to recognize themselves as merely the instruments through which the call of Christ and of his Spirit comes to effect. The Church is acting *ministerially* in doing the will of Christ. The word of Paul to the elders of Ephesus is surely relevant to this fact: "Take heed to yourselves and to all the flock, in which the Holy Spirit hath made you bishops, to shepherd the church of God, which he hath purchased with his own blood" (Acts 20:28).

When these two facts are coordinated, namely, the permanency of the gifts which qualify for the office, and the judgment of the church that Christ is calling this man to the exercise of the office, it seems to me quite inconsistent with all that is implicit in the judgment and action of the church, for the person in question to be ordained and installed in the office for a limited term. In the absence of any express warrant for term eldership it is, to say the least, most precarious to assume that ordination for a limited term is legitimate. When we duly assess the weight of the consideration that the gifts which qualify for the office are the gifts of Christ, and therefore in effect the call of Christ and of his Spirit to the exercise of these gifts, when we bear in mind that the possession of these gifts is not temporary but abiding, and that the gifts increase in fruitfulness and effectiveness with their exercise, the most conclusive warrant for ordination to temporary office would have to be provided in order to justify that kind of ordination. It is precisely that conclusive warrant that is lacking. It is in this light that the absence of express warrant takes on the greatest significance. Only conclusive warrant can offset the cogency of these considerations with which we have been dealing.

Finally, there is the argument that pertains to the unity of the office of ruling. In respect of ruling in the church of God, the ruling elder and the teaching elder are on complete parity. When the teaching elder is ordained, he is ordained to rule as well as to teach, and his ruling function is just as permanent as is his teaching function. In the Orthodox Presbyterian Church there is no provision for term ordination of teaching elders, nor has it ever been proposed, as far as I am aware. Term ordination for ruling elders has been proposed and contended for. There is surely some inconsistency here. To say the least, consistency would appear to demand that, if term eldership is approved and provided for in our Form of Government in the case of ruling elders, the same should be approved and provided for in the case of teaching elders.

It will perhaps help to point up the anomaly of term eldership when we think of the same type of ordination in the case of teaching elders. No doubt the reason why the latter has not been seriously proposed is that it appears incompatible with the calling which teaching eldership implies, that is, the call to the gospel ministry. Exactly so! When the call to ruling eldership is properly weighed, and its implications properly evaluated, we should have the same sense of incompatibility in thinking of term eldership in the case of ruling elders.

The most important consideration of all in this connection is that term eldership for ruling elders draws a line of cleavage between ruling elders and teaching elders in respect of that one function which is common to both, and in terms of which both are on complete parity. The teaching elder is ordained to permanent tenure of the ruling office, the ruling elder would not be if the practice of term eldership is adopted. Here is a line of distinction which tends to institute a sharp cleavage between the ruling elder and the teaching elder in respect of that one thing where it is necessary to preserve unity and complete parity. One cannot but feel that the practice of term eldership for ruling elders is but a hangover of an unwholesome clericalism which has failed to recognize the basic unity of the office of elder and, particularly, the complete parity of all elders in the matter of government.

If it should be argued that the minister is called to a life work, and makes labour in the Word and doctrine his exclusive, full-time employment, whereas the ruling elder does not, there are these things to be said:

1. Granted that the minister gives all his time to this task, and the elder does not, it by no means follows that the elder need not be regarded as called to the permanent discharge of the office of ruling. He may not devote all his time to it, but there is absolutely no evidence that he is not called to it as a permanent office. Full-time and part-time have absolutely nothing to do with the question of the permanency of the call to office.

2. I Tim. 5:17 indicates that the ruling elder is to be remuneratively rewarded for his labour in ruling. The call to part-time remunerative labour has as much claim to permanence as full-time remunerative labour.

3. Even ruling elders may devote all their time to the ruling and pastoral duties, and be remunerated accordingly. The labourer is worthy of his hire.

Practical Considerations against Term Eldership

1. It tends to create in the minds of the people the notion of trial periods. That should have no place whatsoever in the election of elders.
2. It tends to develop such a notion in the minds of elders themselves, and therefore a decreased sense of responsibility and office.
3. It interferes with the continuity, and therefore with the sense of responsibility, as also with the stability of the office.

4. It may occasion the removal of good elders as well as bad ones.
5. It may minister to party division and strife.
6. It is rather liable to give the impression of representative government and of democracy. Presbyterianism is not democratic.
7. It tends to promote the idea that the eldership should be passed around.

In conclusion there is no sound practical argument that may be advanced that cannot be offset by a multiplicity of practical arguments on the other side.

INDEX OF SCRIPTURE

On the following pages are some resources produced by P&R Publishing that will help you in your shepherding ministry.

For a full catalog write to:

P&R Publishing
PO Box 817
Phillipsburg, NJ 08865
Telephone 800-631-0094

Or visit our website, www.prpbooks.com

Reformed Expository Commentaries

"Those of us who regularly preach need commentaries that provide the best biblical scholarship and also understand the practical challenges of today's pastorate. The Reformed Expository Commentary series, prepared by Reformed preachers of great scholarly ability, ably speaks to both needs. As combined exegetical and homiletical commentaries, they are a sermon preparation text of exceptional value. The authors of the Westminster Confession of Faith advised pastors to speak to both 'the necessities and capacities' of our people. This commentary series, which so well understands God's Word and God's people, greatly aids in that dual task of faithful preachers."

—Bryan Chapell, President, Covenant Seminary, St. Louis, MO

Esther and Ruth, Iain M. Duguid, 978-0-87552-783-3
Daniel, Iain M. Duguid, 978-1-59638-068-4
Zechariah, Richard D. Phillips, 978-1-59638-028-8
Matthew (2 vol. set), Daniel M. Doriani, 978-1-59638-151-3
Luke (2 vol. set), Philip Graham Ryken, 978-1-59638-152-0
Galatians, Philip Graham Ryken, 978-0-87552-782-6
Ephesians, Bryan Chapell, 978-1-59638-016-5
1 Timothy, Philip Graham Ryken, 978-1-59638-049-3
Hebrews, Richard D. Phillips, 978-0-87552-784-0
James, Daniel M. Doriani, 978-0-87552-785-7
The Incarnation in the Gospels; Daniel M. Doriani, Richard D. Phillips, Philip Graham Ryken; 978-1-59638-140-7

Living Word BIBLE STUDIES

by Kathleen Buswell Nielson

  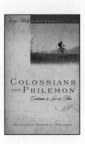 

"With rich insight and wisdom, Kathleen Nielson invites her students 'to grapple with the text' as she provides helpful contexts and comments along with stimulating study questions. Kathleen's studies are good food for the soul—challenging, convicting, and very, very encouraging."

> —**Carol Ruvolo,** Author of 13 Bible study books and
> Founder of JoyPals Network

Joshua: All God's Good Promises, 978-1-59638-105-6
Psalms: Songs Along the Way, 978-1-59638-148-3
Proverbs: The Ways of Wisdom, 978-1-59638-081-3
Ecclesiastes & Song of Songs: Wisdom's Searching and Finding,
   978-1-59638-149-0
Colossians and Philemon: Continue to Live in Him,
   978-1-59638-073-8
1 & 2 Thessalonians: Living the Gospel to the End,
   978-1-59638-104-9

Explorations in Biblical Theology

Robert A. Peterson, Series Editor

  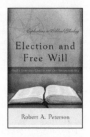 

"Neither superficial nor highly technical, this new series of volumes on important Christian doctrines is projected to teach Reformed theology as it is most helpfully taught, with clear grounding in Scripture, mature understanding of theology, gracious interaction with others who disagree, and useful application to life. I expect that these volumes will strengthen the faith and biblical maturity of all who read them, and I am happy to recommend them highly."

—**Wayne Grudem**, Research Professor of Bible and Theology, Phoenix Seminary, Phoenix, AZ

Anointed with the Spirit and Power: The Holy Spirit's Empowering Presence, John D. Harvey, 978-1-59638-017-2

The Elder: Today's Ministry Rooted in All of Scripture, Cornelis Van Dam, 978-1-59638-141-4

Election and Free Will: God's Gracious Choice and Our Responsibility, Robert A. Peterson, 978-0-87552-793-2

The Nearness of God: His Presence with His People, J. Lanier Burns, 978-1-59638-056-1

Our Secure Salvation: Preservation and Apostasy, Robert A. Peterson, 978-1-59638-043-1

The Gospel According to the Old Testament

"One of the most urgent needs of the church is to grasp how the many parts of the Bible fit together to make one 'story-line' that culminates in Jesus Christ. This series of books goes a long way toward meeting that need. Written at a thoughtful but popular level, it deserves wide circulation."

—**D. A. Carson**, Trinity Evangelical Divinity School, Deerfield, IL

Basics of the Faith

"Those who teach and lead will love these booklets because they are a perfect resource to share with inquirers and to use in discipleship. Church members will love them because they supply meaty and understandable instruction in important aspects of Christian doctrine, duty, and devotion."

—**J. Ligon Duncan III**, Senior Minister, First Presbyterian Church, Jackson, MS

How Do We Glorify God?, John D. Hannah, 978-1-59638-082-0
How Our Children Come to Faith, Stephen Smallman,
   978-1-59638-053-0
What Are Election and Predestination?, Richard D. Phillips,
   978-1-59638-045-5
What Is a Reformed Church?, Stephen Smallman, 978-0-87552-594-5
What Is a True Calvinist?, Philip Graham Ryken, 978-0-87552-598-3
What Is Biblical Preaching?, Eric J. Alexander, 978-1-59638-113-1
What Is Church Government?, Sean Michael Lucas,
   978-1-59638-150-6
What Is Justification by Faith Alone?, J. V. Fesko, 978-1-59638-083-7
What Is Perseverance of the Saints?, Michael A. Milton,
   978-1-59638-150-6
What Is Providence?, Derek W. H. Thomas, 978-1-59638-092-9
What Is Spiritual Warfare?, Stanley D. Gale, 978-1-59638-123-0
What Is the Christian Worldview?, Philip Graham Ryken,
   978-1-59638-008-0
What Is the Lord's Supper?, Richard D. Phillips, 978-0-87552-647-8
What Is True Conversion?, Stephen Smallman, 978-0-87552-659-1
Why Do We Baptize Infants?, Bryan Chapell, 978-1-59638-058-5

Resources for Biblical Living

 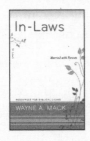  

"Biblical, practical, straightforward, and timely are the main qualities that these brief booklets will offer to those who read them. If you're looking for a relevant word for your difficult path, read them hopefully and receive much needed direction."
—**Lance Quinn**, President, National Association of Nouthetic Counselors

Bitterness: The Root That Pollutes, Lou Priolo, 978-1-59638-130-8

Deception: Letting Go of Lying, Lou Priolo, 978-1-59638-129-2

Divorce: Before You Say "I Don't", Lou Priolo, 978-1-59638-078-3

Fear: Breaking Its Grip, Lou Priolo, 978-1-59638-121-6

In-Laws: Married with Parents, Wayne A. Mack, 978-1-59638-170-4

Judgments: Rash or Righteous, Lou Priolo, 978-1-59638-120-9

Manipulation: Knowing How to Respond, Lou Priolo,
    978-1-59638-128-5

Motherhood: Hope for Discouraged Moms, Brenda Payne,
    978-1-59638-169-8

Problems: Solving Them God's Way, Jay E. Adams, 978-1-59638-184-1

Self-Image: How to Overcome Inferiority Judgments, Lou Priolo,
    978-1-59638-079-0

Resources for Changing Lives

Small booklets on single-issue subjects that have been proven to help counselors achieve lasting resolutions. Produced in association with the Christian Counseling & Education Foundation (C.C.E.F.)

ADD, Welch, 978-0-87552-676-8

Anger, Powlison, 978-0-87552-681-2

Angry at God?, Jones, 978-0-87552-691-1

Bad Memories, Jones, 978-0-87552-661-4

Depression, Welch, 978-0-87552-682-9

Domestic Abuse, Powlison/Tripp/ Welch, 978-0-87552-687-4

Forgiveness, Jones, 978-0-87552-678-2

God's Love, Powlison, 978-0-87552-686-7

Guidance, Petty, 978-0-87552-694-2

Homosexuality, Welch, 978-0-87552-683-6

Just One More, Welch, 978-0-87552-689-8

Marriage, Tripp, 978-0-87552-675-1

Motives, Welch, 978-0-87552-692-8

OCD, Emlet, 978-0-87552-698-0

Pornography, Powlison, 978-0-87552-677-5

Pre-Engagement, Powlison/Yenchko, 978-0-87552-679-9

Priorities, Petty, 978-0-87552-685-0

Procrastination, Henegar, 978-0-87552-699-7

Self-Injury, Welch, 978-0-87552-697-3

Sexual Sin, Black, 978-0-87552-690-4

Stress, Powlison, 978-0-87552-660-7

Suffering, Tripp, 978-0-87552-684-3

Suicide, Black, 978-0-87552-693-5

Teens and Sex, Tripp, 978-0-87552-680-5

Thankfulness, Lutz, 978-0-87552-688-1

Why Me? Powlison, 978-0-87552-695-9

Worry, Powlison, 978-0-87552-696-6